SOLDIERS
ONCE

SOLDIERS
ONCE

MY BROTHER

AND THE

LOST
DREAMS

OF

AMERICA'S
VETERANS

CATHERINE WHITNEY

DA CAPO PRESS
A Member of the Perseus Books Group

Designed by Pauline Brown
Set in 12 point Berkeley by the Perseus Books Group

Library of Congress Cataloging-in-Publication Data

Whitney, Catherine.
  Soldiers once : my brother and the lost dreams of America's veterans / Catherine Whitney.
     p. cm.
  Includes bibliographical references and index.
  ISBN 978-0-306-81788-5
  1. Schuler, James Walter, d. 2001. 2. Vietnam War, 1961–1975—Veterans—United States. 3. Veterans—United States—Biography.
4. Veterans—United States—Social conditions. 5. Veterans—United States—Mental health. 6. Veterans—Services for—United States.
7. Whitney, Catherine—Family. 8. Brothers—United States—Biography.
I. Title.
  DS559.73.U6W47 2009
  305.9'0697092—dc22
  [B]
                                                            2008048683

Published by Da Capo Press
A Member of the Perseus Books Group
www.dacapopress.com

Da Capo Press books are available at special discounts for bulk purchases in the U.S. by corporations, institutions, and other organizations. For more information, please contact the Special Markets Department at the Perseus Books Group, 2300 Chestnut Street, Suite 200, Philadelphia, PA 19103, or call (800) 810-4145, ext. 5000, or e-mail special.markets@perseusbooks.com.

10 9 8 7 6 5 4 3 2 1

For Jim
1948–2001

CONTENTS

ACKNOWLEDGMENTS

T HIS HAS NOT been an easy story to tell, and it would not have made it into print without the unfaltering belief and support of many people. Chief among these was my agent, Jane Dystel, who wouldn't give up, even as many publishing companies rejected the topic as "too negative" or too difficult to face. Jane wouldn't let go, and she eventually found an editor who shared her passion. Robert Pigeon at Da Capo Press, a veteran himself, immediately grasped the power of a narrative that is both haunting and hopeful. He has been a guiding force as I shaped the book.

I feel undying gratitude toward my partner, Paul Krafin, whose understanding of military culture and deep compassion for those who serve, contributed a level of insight I couldn't have managed on my own. Paul is also a wonderful writer, and he made a positive mark on this book.

My family has been a meaningful part of this process. After all, it is their story, too. In particular, I am grateful to my sister Joanne Laha, who was so instrumental in researching material for the book; and to my mother, Janet Schuler, without whose endorsement this story could never have been written. I am thankful to my other siblings and their families, who shared memories and offered insight during the process: Greg and Sherry Schuler, Paul and Marci Schuler, Tom Schuler, Mary Lattier, John Schuler, Margaret Schuler and her husband, Tsegahun Tessema, and Joanne's husband, Tom Laha.

My son, Paul, has served as a reliable link to the younger generation and has pressed me throughout this process to reach for a true portrait of my brother. "I want to know Uncle Jim," he said. "The good side of him, the real Jim." I hope I've achieved it. I was always glad to have Paul's input, and his wife, Sophie's, too.

In writing *Soldiers Once*, I join the community of people who have demonstrated time and again their commitment to our soldiers and veterans. I am proud to be a part of this noble cause, and I would like to single out several people who have been especially helpful to me: Greg Mitchell, Jerry Donnellan, Jeff Wilson, Paul Rieckhoff, Jay Hirsch, and Senator Jim Webb.

I reserve my deepest gratitude for the veterans themselves— those who reached across the barriers of time and distance, all of the strangers who offered their help in my search for my brother. In particular, I am thankful to William L. Smith, John Walker, Richard Hauer, Christian Burton, Fred Mukowsky, David Orr, and Jim Keenan. You were the best and brightest once, and, in my view, you are even more so today.

Finally, I want to raise a tribute to my late father, Richard Schuler. He was a patriot and a man of peace, and under his tutelage I learned that love is the great conquering force of human existence. Thanks, Dad.

˙ARMCHAIR PATRIOTS

Every Saturday I do my weekly shopping along Route 59, a major thoroughfare in Rockland County, New York, where I live. It's a busy strip, identical to countless others across the country, cluttered with the usual collection of discount outlets, strip malls, and big-box stores. During the past five years, as I've approached the major intersection at Middletown Road, I have been jolted from my idle thoughts to confront a central question of our national life.

For more than three hundred weeks now, two separate groups, each numbering forty or fifty people, have gathered on the opposite corners of the intersection. The first group waves signs that read: "Honk if you support the troops." The second group waves signs that read: "Honk to end the war." As the drivers around me pound their car horns with certainty—*Yes!* to the troops, *Yes!* to peace—I freeze every time, sliding silently by, annoyed, confused, and embarrassed. I have the same thought week after week: "What the hell? That's not a choice. *I* support the troops. *I* support peace. Why should I have to pick one over the other?"

That's what we've come to, shouting slogans. Slogans are truly the opiate of the masses. They tug at the heart and confer certitude in uncertain times. They allow an armchair war to play out for those of us whose toughest challenges don't come at the point of a rifle. And they are utterly false.

The question of what it means to support the troops has been much on my mind since the death of my brother Jim in 2001. He was a soldier once, whose heroic service in Vietnam was followed by a long and steady decline. His lonely death at age fifty-three was the silent coda, the quiet fall to earth of a warrior who succumbed to his wounds many years after his last battle had been fought. Although it's true that many of our veterans return from war to wonderful lives of great productivity and success, others never recover, physically or emotionally, and Jim was one of those. In particular, Jim's war has come to symbolize the plight of the lost soldier, broken by the effects of post-traumatic stress disorder, substance abuse, and poverty. The average age at which a Vietnam veteran dies is fifty-six years old—a good twenty years earlier than his nonveteran counterparts.

It would be an oversimplification to say that Jim's problems were seeded and took root in Vietnam alone—or that the blame for his early death can be laid entirely at the military's feet. But there are central truths in Jim's story, truths we must face, about the culture of indifference that allows us on the one hand to honk our horns in support of the troops, and on the other to completely ignore them when they return from battle.

For here we are fighting another war, and the soldiers are coming home to face even greater challenges, while our nation's mentality is stuck in the yellow ribbon phase.

There is a significant disconnect between what we say about supporting our troops and what we actually do to support them. We seem to despise the weakness of the wounded soldier, especially when it is manifested by mental illness, social alienation, or undefined degenerative diseases caused by exposure to Agent Orange or by Gulf War syndrome. It isn't just the politicians. It's all of us. We embrace our brothers when they first return from war, and then we ask them to pack away their medals and their pain, and move on. Watching the news one night, I heard a woman articulate what I know many people feel about Vietnam veterans: "The war has been over for thirty years," she said, exasperated. "Can't we put Vietnam behind us?"

Clearly we can't. The wounds of an unexamined war still fester, flaring up every few years with stunning emotional pain. There will be no end to Vietnam until we make an effort to heal those wounds. To do that we must pay attention to the uncounted number of veterans who live on our streets, reside in our hospitals, and barely subsist in isolation and poverty across the country. At the same time, we must pledge that we will take care of a new generation of soldiers who will be returning to our communities by the hundreds of thousands in the coming years.

This book is about my brother Jim, but beyond his story, it's about how we can make good on our promise of support to these young men and women—not in the immediacy of war, but in its long, slow aftermath. We are a nation exhilarated by battle but indifferent to the requirements of peace. Our memories of war's sacrifices are brief, our good will as fleeting as the puff of smoke from the muzzle of a rifle that begins to evaporate the moment it strikes the air. The yellow ribbons tatter and darken with time, disappearing from the trees as normal life resumes. Today's war heroes too often become tomorrow's poor, many living in run-down apartment complexes around military bases, where they have PX privileges and can squeeze out discounts for their essential needs.

Our hearts may swell with pride as we watch our men and women at war, but we seem unable to give them peace with dignity.

I embarked on writing this book concerned that I was treading on sacred ground, going places I had no right to be. In truth, I am a terribly inadequate messenger. I am a woman who has never experienced war, a pampered civilian who has never exhibited a single act of physical courage, unless you count giving birth. I don't pretend to understand the experience of war. Many of the veterans I spoke with stared at me with hard, suspicious eyes or condescending smiles, aware of this fact and not fully trusting that I would be able to understand their stories. Their distrust was warranted; I'm the first to admit it. But still. I have been enlightened by my engagement with these men. When my brother was alive, I could not understand nor accept his torment. In the aftermath of his death, I chose to look at him with eyes wide open. I was blind, but now I see—and having seen, I act in the only way I know how. I write about it. I say, in effect, "Come on, people now, smile on your brothers." Support the troops. No, love them. Give them their due.

If we, the people, don't do this, no one will.

Our brothers, husbands, wives, fathers, mothers, uncles, aunts, friends, and countrymen—millions strong, millions weak—have served their nation, while we, the armchair patriots, have rested on the laurels that they planted and nurtured. We can argue about whether or not each war has been a good war or a just war. It doesn't matter. Still, they served.

This book is for them.

Those whose victories in the great wars saved the world but left scars within that they couldn't acknowledge.

Those who came home from an Asian nightmare that the nation wanted to forget, and became the lost generation;

Those who sacrificed limbs and eyes and pieces of their souls;

Those who fought in wars the people at home called mistakes.

They were soldiers once—and now?

That is up to us.

TAPS

WITH THE THANKS OF A GRATEFUL NATION

MY BROTHER JIM was buried with full military honors on September 10, 2001, at Tahoma Memorial Cemetery in Kent, Washington.

It was a brilliantly sunny day, the sky deep blue, the air washed clean by an early drizzle. The stark, snow-covered peak of Mount Rainier stood at majestic sentry. Rows of grey tombstones lined the deep green expanse of the cemetery as far as the eye could see, their spines erect in the hard earth.

James Walter Schuler, staff sergeant, United States Army, retired, was fifty-three years old when he died.

We were a small group, seated on wooden folding chairs overlooking a tree-shaded lawn. It was mostly family—our mother and her eight remaining children. Dad had been gone five years by then, his own flag-draped coffin long in the grave. He was a navy man, and his World War II experiences had been relegated to a few sentimental memories and a framed photo of his ship that hung in our living room.

But Jim's journey had been different, his life and death complicated by war wounds that penetrated far deeper than the pieces of shrapnel that won him his Purple Heart. Jim might have rested more easily had his death come in a moment of combat, rather than unceremoniously in a lonely apartment.

Perhaps we would have cried less bitter tears, strangely happy to be able to call Jim a hero. But it hadn't happened that way. Heroics performed during forgotten missions in the jungles of Vietnam were decades old, and the man we buried was long past the time when anyone saw him as a valiant warrior.

In our close-knit family, Jim was the snapped cord, the missing link, a man in hiding from his own people. Now we shifted uneasily in our seats as we gathered to lay Jim to rest. It had been sixteen years since any of us had seen him, and for most of that time we didn't know where he was. His sporadic letters to our mother often bore no return address. We told ourselves he had abandoned us. We argued with our consciences, saying that he could have reached out at any time, insisting that we wanted him to. But it wasn't true. We were tense in his presence, afraid of the simmering rage that sparked so suddenly when Jim drank. The last time we were all together, he had been violent. We were relieved when he left.

Unwilling to take any further action ourselves, we found it easy to blame the army, which we viewed as Jim's surrogate family. After all, they had been the ones who'd taken him in. He had volunteered, and the army had accepted him. He'd been a lifer—twenty years in the service of his nation.

We expected the army to behave as a stern but loving parent, to rein Jim in, to cure him of his addictions and to temper his demons. This justification now seemed hollow. How could we think an enormous, faceless bureaucracy would hold our brother close, not only cleanse but reconstitute him, when we ourselves could and would not?

I glanced at my mother, seated beside me, her face an impenetrable mask of sorrow. But I knew precisely what was going on. She was tormenting herself, taking the blame for Jim's failings, cataloging the mistakes she'd made as her thoughts flipped through the calendar pages of his troubled life. She shouldn't have done so, but she was unable to stop herself. Your child is still your child, even when he is fifty-three years old, and guilt is a persistent demon. In tormented reflection, life's script never stops being written and rewritten, each time with a different ending, even as the finality of the coffin sits in silent judgment only feet away.

I'm sure Mom rationally understood that the struggles of Jim's life and his sad, early death weren't her fault. Nevertheless, there he was. And so, at last, she had failed him. In the long shadows cast by time and eroded by memory, logic fails, and so does wisdom. The heart will not be convinced. Every parent carries that special burden.

We listened to the prayerful drone of the priest. I stared down at the funeral program, whose cover featured the childhood photo of a redheaded imp wearing a devilish, toothy grin. We had chosen to memorialize Jim not as the stranger he had become, but as the boy we had once known.

Sweet, sweet childhood. When the end looms, the mind reaches back to the comfort of a time closer to the beginning. Those were the easy years, when my siblings and I were free to roam on long, lazy summer days—running through the sprinkler that was a fixture in our backyard, eating peaches straight from the tree, picking berries in the overgrown patches next to the railroad tracks, waiting for Dad to drive up in his milk truck so we could all cram inside its cold, galvanized-steel-walled world, comforted by the rhythmic clank of empty return bottles in loose cases, and the cool texture of the slick floor awash with melting ice. Our traumas then were no worse than a bee sting on a bare foot or a sliver of wood embedded in a pink thumb. I'm sure my mother's memory lingered on those times. It was irresistible. She wanted her child back, the darling boy in the photo, but he had been gone for a long time, his innocent, open face re-placed by a darker, brooding visage. Her handsome son had dis-appeared to a place where she couldn't reach him.

As the last plaintive note of Taps echoed across the field, the honor guard—three young men resplendent in their dress uniforms—raised their rifles toward the open skies and split the air with three loud cracks.

"Jim would have loved this," my sister Joanne murmured, and we all shared a smile. It was one thing we knew for sure about our brother—his love of pageantry and the pride he took in his military identity. How pleased he would have been to see these fine young men with their formal bearing, their crisp uni-forms, their obedience to honor, firing clean blasts into the air to send off their fellow soldier. It was a secular ritual, but it felt holy.

A small, silent man hung toward the back at Jim's funeral, and he approached our mother after the ceremony. "Mrs. Schuler," he said shyly, "I came to pay my respects."

Eddie Rose had been a scrawny kid, and he was a thin, ropey adult, barely five foot seven. His face had a battered, seen-it-all look, but his shaggy brown hair didn't have a touch of gray, and his toothy grin was remarkably similar to the one he had worn as a boy. Eddie was Jim's best childhood friend, and the two boys were inseparable. They joined the army at around the same time and, remarkably, were assigned to the same battalion at one point in Vietnam.

We were thrilled to see Eddie, and we hoped he could provide some answers about Jim. He agreed to join us later at Mom's house, but he never showed up. Later, when I tried to track him down, I couldn't find him. He had disappeared back into the silence—a pattern I would find to be very common among Vietnam veterans.

After the service, we made the long drive back to our mother's house in Seattle, where we busied ourselves with food and drink and the familiar loud conversations that were a trademark of our clan's gatherings.

There is a wall in Mom's house, right off the living room, decorated with framed pictures of each of her children, in the order of their birth. Airbrushed high-school graduation portraits—the kind that look a little too perfect, cheeks a little too pink, eyes a little too blue.

Jim's portrait stood out from the rest. There had been no high-school graduation for him; instead, he had joined the army. So, there was a picture of seventeen-year-old Jim in his military uniform. His thick red hair had been close-cropped. His chiseled face was set in determination. His eyes glowed with fervor, but it was something other than innocence that emanated from them. In his uniform, he looked much older than his age.

We ate, drank, laughed, and performed the full theater of "remember the time," carefully choosing memories, skirting the fresher mysteries in favor of the beach scenes, ballgames, and innocent troublemaking of our youth.

It wasn't our family's way to pick at scabs. But in the days after we buried Jim, we might have settled in as a family and begun the task of figuring out exactly what had happened to him. We might have taken the time to contemplate Jim's premature death—the way his life had begun to unravel on the fields of Vietnam thirty years earlier, and had kept unraveling after he'd finally done his twenty years and retired, like a long, slow death march toward alcoholism, poverty, and isolation.

We might have searched for a way to explain why a twenty-year veteran of the United States Army, who had served three tours of duty in Vietnam and collected a drawer full of medals, could have nothing to show for it but a small ceremony in a military graveyard and a ritually folded triangle of flag laid to rest in his mother's arms.

We might have spent time in those days after we buried Jim going through the single box of belongings we'd retrieved from his tiny apartment in Killeen, Texas. We might have studied each medal and award, each letter of commendation detailing the heroics performed.

But we never had a chance. Another kind of tragedy intervened.

The day after Jim's funeral, I awoke before dawn. My flight to New York was scheduled to leave from Sea-Tac Airport at 8:00 A.M., and my mind had shifted from thoughts of my brother to my life back home.

Kissing my mother good-bye, I sped off in my rental car for the airport. The drive was pleasantly familiar, one I'd taken dozens of times over the years—blowing down the I-5 in the first red light of morning's dawn. Seattle was beautiful at that hour. I loved the way the sun's early glow spotlighted the Space Needle. It never failed to remind me of a dictum often repeated by my father, the navy man:

Red sky at night, sailors delight.
Red sky in the morning, sailors take warning.

The radio was on, and as I neared the car-rental return, I heard that a small plane had flown into the World Trade Center. I barely gave it a thought beyond how awful, how pointless. Minutes later, I was in line at the Delta gate. It was 6:00 A.M. in Seattle; 9:00 A.M. in New York.

Everyone has precise and vivid memories of that morning. Mine involve an agitated man standing behind me in the check-in line. He tapped me on the shoulder and asked if he could go ahead of me, as he was late for his flight. I stood aside, and he rushed forward to the ticket counter. Later, I would think of him, hurrying to go nowhere. By the time I reached the counter, the agents were clumped in a whispering huddle. Something was up. One of them broke away and approached me, a sallow woman with a worried frown line sketched into her brow who gasped when she saw my destination. "There's a problem in New York," she said. "Please step aside."

Irritated, I stupidly remarked, "Oh, you mean the small plane that hit the World Trade Center. That's miles away from the airport . . ."

Just at that moment, the area around me erupted in a babble of excitement and alarm. I wandered toward a wall-mounted TV, where a crowd of passengers watched plumes of thick black smoke rising from the Twin Towers.

My cell phone buzzed. It was my mother. "Come home," she cried. "They're attacking America."

And so we never had a chance to fully contemplate the significance of Jim's life, or the tragedy of his death. On September 11, 2001, Jim was blown from our thoughts with the explosive force of two airliners crashing into the twin towers of the World Trade Center. A new war was engaged, with an army of fresh names and faces. Banners unfurled in the windows of stores and on the bumpers of SUVs. They fluttered giddily in the air across freeway overpasses. The familiar chant spilled out from the soul of a nation blind to its meaning: *Support our troops*.

ONE

FINAL
JOURNEY
HOME

2001

HE HAD BEEN DEAD for three days before they found him. Despite the heavy August heat that had settled over central Texas, it took time for the odor of decay to seep out from under a thin crack in the apartment door. The building manager, Liz, whose apartment was next to his on the ground floor, recognized that sweet, sickening smell. She was familiar with the way it clogged the senses and permeated the skin so that it was still there after a dozen vigorous scrubbings. With a shaking hand, she picked up the phone and dialed 911.

When the officers arrived, Liz handed them her master key and stood back, pressing a handkerchief to her nose and mouth as they opened the door. Her tenant, James Schuler—she always called him James, never Jim—was slumped in a chair in front of an old black-and-white TV, his graying red hair haloed with a swarm of flies. His face was bloated and discolored, a dark purple, almost black. His eyes were open. Liz turned away and went outside, where she inhaled deep gulps of fresh, hot air.

Over the next two hours, as police and medical personnel busied themselves inside the apartment, Liz sat on a plastic lawn chair next to the building's small swimming pool. Normally, children would be leaping and splashing in the tepid water, trying to fend off the oppressive heat. Not today. As the afternoon progressed, several tenants joined Liz, talking and smoking as they watched the flurry of activity.

Like most of the residents of the forty-unit apartment building, Liz was black. She had been married to a career army man who'd served in Vietnam, and when he died in 1992, she'd stayed on, supplementing her widow's benefits with the part-time manager's job. James wasn't the first resident to die in his apartment since Liz had been manager, but he was by far the youngest. Wiping away tears, Liz confided to the others that she would miss the quiet man with the shy manner and easy smile. They nodded. Everyone had been fond of James.

Finally, a stretcher emerged from the apartment, the body bundled tight and secured with belts. It was loaded into a waiting ambulance, and the little group continued its vigil as the lights of the vehicle disappeared into the distance. One of the police officers who had been first on the scene ambled over and pulled out a notebook. He was young and well muscled, as if he'd just come from lifting weights in a gym. His face, damp with sweat, was unlined and boyish—a baby face on a man's body.

"A few questions, ma'am," he addressed Liz in a deep drawl. She nodded. She had already identified the body earlier, confirming that it was that of her tenant, James Schuler. Now the officer wanted to know when she'd last seen him alive. She'd been trying to remember that very thing all afternoon. Usually, she saw James every day. He kept a regular schedule, appearing in pressed slacks and shirt, freshly showered and shaved, around 11:00 each morning. She knew he took walks, and he sometimes played golf. Twice a week he swept the complex's two parking lots, for which Liz gave him a modest discount on his $375 rent. Sometimes he would linger by the pool and chat with Liz and the other tenants.

Liz told the officer that she hadn't seen James for a couple of days. Normally, she would have noticed, but she'd been distracted by problems in the building. No, she said, she didn't know any of his friends. He pretty much kept to himself.

"Family?" the officer asked.

"He has family out west," she said. "I think Washington State. I don't believe they were close."

The phone rang in our mother's house in Seattle at 8:45 A.M., with the news that her second-born son was dead of an apparent heart attack. For several moments after the call, she sat by the phone, bearing the awful news alone, wishing her husband of fifty years, who had died in 1996, was there to share it, and then immediately feeling relief that he would not have to experience the loss. The death of a child, even one in his fifties, is a blow like no other, a cruel reversal of the natural order of things.

Mom had never stopped blaming herself for her son's alienation. On his last visit home, sixteen years earlier, Jim had drunkenly accused her of not loving him the way she loved her other children. Since then, her obsession, which would become somewhat more pronounced after his death, was to pore over the events of Jim's childhood, putting her actions under a microscope, trying to pinpoint the moment in time when she had failed him. We all tried to convince her that it was a futile exercise. She had raised nine children, and the rest of us were living witnesses to her devotion. It seemed obvious that Jim's problems had more complex roots, but our mother could not shake the sense that she was to blame.

I was at my desk in my home office in New York when the phone rang. "I have some sad news," Mom said, her voice trembling a little. "Jim is dead."

My first reaction was a strange lack of surprise, a sense that an inevitable end had been reached. But following my mother's call, I felt unsettled and unable to work. The grief built like a slow wave in the ensuing hours, as the reality began to sink in. My thoughts kept returning to Jim—not the Jim who had died mysteriously in Killeen, Texas, a man I didn't know, living in a place I'd never been. It was a younger Jim I recalled, handsome in his uniform, his thick hair burnished a deep red, the crooked smile and sea-foam blue eyes, so pale they seemed to disappear. My mental snapshot was circa 1966, the year Jim went to war.

It was agreed that our brother Tom would go to Killeen to make arrangements for Jim's body to be shipped home, to retrieve his possessions, and to find out what he could of his life there. Tom was a dispatcher for a taxi company in Anchorage, and he had some vacation time coming. He volunteered for the grim mission, and the rest of us were glad to let him go.

Tom had only been ten years old when Jim first went to war, and he had looked up to his brother with awe. But he, too, had lost touch with him, and he felt a lot of guilt about that. For the past couple of years, Tom had been talking about taking a trip to Texas to find Jim. He'd get in his old car and rumble across the West—down the coast to California, through the desert into Arizona, and finally to Texas. He was convinced that once in Killeen, he would be able to find Jim. He liked to imagine how he'd walk up to his brother, maybe on a golf course, or show up at his door as casually as if he lived down the street. "Hey, bro," he'd say, and Jim would be shocked, but he'd smile that big toothy grin.

"I pictured us sitting down and having a long talk," Tom said dreamily. "I'd tell him that I had the utmost respect for him. I wanted to thank him for his service in the military. And I wanted to finally end the confusion and bad feelings. It was a guilt trip on my part, for sure."

In his fantasy, Tom imagined staying for a few days and getting to know his brother again before returning to Seattle, where he would give Mom the good news about how well Jim was doing—tanned and relaxed, playing golf, hanging out with friends, chasing women, supplementing his retirement pay with a good part-time job. It seemed like a wonderful plan.

Now it was too late. Tom called me before he boarded the plane to Austin. "I feel like shit," he said, in his low, gravely voice. "I really blew it, Catherine."

"We all blew it," I told him, struck again by the finality of our loss. It had been on the back burner for all of us. Someday we'd rescue Jim from the jungle of his self-destruction and bring him home. We'd pin those medals back on his chest and honor him like we should have done thirty years earlier. He died waiting for us to show up.

The temperature was in the high nineties when Tom's plane touched down in Austin. He rented a car and set off on the sixty-mile drive north to Killeen. The humidity seemed to warp the highway with its heavy pressure, and thunderstorms broke out several times as he drove.

Once a sleepy, cotton-farming town of twelve thousand people, Killeen was transformed into a busy military center in the 1950s when Fort Hood and Robert Gray Air Force Base became permanent installations. Today the massive base stretches over 340 miles and accommodates a post population of 71,000: 42,000 soldiers, their families, and civilian employees. The adjacent city of Killeen houses thousands more. Many, like Jim, are veterans, staying close to the base to take advantage of the permanent PX privileges, and to keep in touch with others just like them who might understand where they're coming from and who they were before they were put out to pasture. Killeen is a town that tries hard to buck itself up in the face of a struggling economy and a transient population whose median income is far lower than the state average, and whose minority underclass is much larger.

On the outskirts of town, Tom checked into a motel for the night. He turned the air-conditioning up to full blast and lay on the bed reading brochures about Killeen and leafing through the *Killeen Daily Herald*. Every so often, a huge flying cockroach would whiz into view, jolting him out of his reverie.

The whole experience seemed surreal to Tom. There had been a time, long ago, when he'd briefly considered following in Jim's footsteps and seeking salvation for his own troubles by joining the army. By then, it was late in the Vietnam War. At seventeen, Tom had been on a five-year tumble, swept up in a counter-culture tsunami that had roared through Seattle with a terrifying flood of change. People were the wreckage left behind. When he was thirteen, Tom had started hanging out in a local park with a gang of hippie wannabes, skipping school, smoking pot, and participating in rowdy street demonstrations that often ended with a blast of choking tear gas.

Tom had always been a sensitive child. Much like Jim, he'd struggled to belong, but he lacked Jim's bravado, and so he grew sad and increasingly remote. Like his dropout compatriots, he didn't know where he was going, and he didn't much care. He wasn't against the Vietnam War, but he wasn't for it either. He wanted to be numb.

The sixties were a long time ago, but the era had left its scars on Tom. He never quite recovered, was never able to get his act together after that. Tom is very bright, with a low-key, gentle personality that people find appealing, especially women. But in spite of the aspirations that pulled him forward, Tom struggled to finish school, and never managed to find a partner, settle down, have kids. He was always moving from one short-term occupation to another. He made his home in Alaska, a land of free thinkers, heavy drinkers, and big dreamers, and tried to disappear into its vastness.

When Tom woke the next day, the heat and humidity were still hanging in the air. He ate a big breakfast at Denny's, and then set off for Jim's apartment. As he entered the Fort Hood area, the signs of economic decline became more pronounced. He passed a couple of miles of rundown buildings, cracked sidewalks, and hole-in-the-wall Spanish bodegas. In all, he counted thirteen pawn shops.

Approaching the long, low buildings of Jim's apartment complex, Tom thought they looked like barracks. He parked in the large concrete lot in the back and followed a sign to the manager's apartment, passing a little swimming pool surrounded by a chain-link fence, where several children were playing.

Liz's door was open, and she was sitting inside with two other women, talking and keeping an eye on the kids in the pool. The three women greeted Tom warmly. They seemed thrilled to meet a member of Jim's family.

Liz was a strong-looking woman, dressed in baggy blue pants and a sleeveless blouse. She had a short Afro and a wide, gap-toothed smile. "James was a lovely man," Liz said sincerely. "We miss him." Tom could see that she meant it.

A second woman, whose shiny round face suggested she might be Filipino, introduced herself as Sandy. She beamed at Tom. "James and I shared a wall," she told him. "He never passed by without saying a friendly hello."

"Do any of you know any more about how Jim died?" Tom asked.

The women exchanged uncomfortable glances. Lena, a large, bosomy black woman, with closely cropped graying hair and a stiff, arthritic manner, rocked in her chair and replied, "The Lord took him, so you tell your mama not to worry. His soul be at rest." The others hummed in agreement.

"Jesus have him now," Sandy murmured.

Tom was struck speechless as it dawned on him that these three women, with their staunch serenity and easy prayerfulness, had probably been the people closest to Jim. The brother he'd known had been flashy and extroverted, drawn to sleek cars and pretty women. As far as he knew, Jim had consciously kept his associations white, yet in his final years he'd settled down in the midst of this poor, black community.

Tom couldn't imagine what his brother had been doing here among these women.

Liz located a key and led him to the door of Jim's apartment. "You'll want to hold your breath when you go in," Liz warned him apologetically. "There's still a smell." Tom tried to breathe through his mouth as she pushed the door open and he stepped into the airless apartment.

The lingering scent of decay mingled with the smell of stale tobacco. The living room was just big enough for a chair, a coffee table, and an old TV. Tom stared at the chair where Jim had spent his final moments. It sagged in the middle, and the stretched fabric was stained and marred with cigarette burns.

He felt sick, and it wasn't from the smell. The apartment was a dump, the kind of place a transient might stay. He had pictured Jim's life so differently. He figured a single man could live reasonably well on a military pension. Showed what he knew.

The bedroom contained a single bed with a stripped, lumpy mattress. There were a few clothes in the closet, an iron, a pair of shoes. Where was Jim's stuff? Where was his dress uniform? His dress boots? Jim had loved his dress uniform with its rows of medals and its insignias. It made him proud and infused him with a dignity he could never manage in civilian clothes. He wouldn't have sold it. Would he have been that low? That desperate?

In the tiny kitchen, a yellowing refrigerator contained a few beers and a bottle of ketchup. A bag of miniature Snickers bars sat on the counter. Tom smiled, remembering Jim's sweet tooth. He opened a drawer next to the sink. It held torn up cigarettes, loose tobacco, and cigarette papers. Tom was surprised that Jim rolled his own smokes, considering how cheap cigarettes were in Texas.

In a lower drawer he found Jim's medals. Tom squatted down and fingered them reverently. The Purple Heart in its velvet box seemed to pulse like a living thing. It was beautiful. The heart was trimmed with gold, a profile of George Washington in the center. Above the heart was a shield set between sprays of green leaves. On the back was a raised bronze heart with the words, "For Military Merit."

There were other badges and medals jammed into the drawer, and Tom took them out one by one to look at them—the Vietnam Service Medal with three bronze stars for Jim's three tours of duty in Vietnam, the Republic of Vietnam Campaign Medal, the Meritorious Service Medal, a Presidential Unit Citation, a Meritorious Unit Commendation, the Army Good Conduct Medal, the Republic of Vietnam Gallantry Cross Unit Citation, an Air Assault Badge, an Overseas Service Medal, and an Army of Occupation Medal for the years Jim had served in Berlin after the Vietnam War.

Tom placed the medals in his bag, and continued his search. But there wasn't much else to find. Other than an old address book that was almost empty, the apartment was completely devoid of personal effects. No letters, photos, books, souvenirs. Nothing made the place Jim's home. It was a monk's cell.

"Where are his golf clubs?" Tom asked suddenly, speaking aloud. Jim was an avid golfer, and in his occasional letters home he'd always written that he was enjoying retirement and golfing every day. There wasn't even a golf tee in his apartment.

Needing air, Tom stepped outside and stood in the doorway of Liz's apartment, where the women were still chatting and laughing. Liz motioned for him to join them, and he stepped in-side and sat down at the kitchen table.

"I was wondering," Tom said, accepting a glass of sweetened iced tea, "whether there are golf clubs. Jim wrote that he golfed a lot. I know he loved to golf. But I didn't find any clubs."

"Oh, James was quite a golfer," Liz answered, nodding and smiling. "The course is just down the road. He walked over there a couple of times a week. I don't know about clubs." She shrugged and repeated, "But he sure loved to golf."

Tom sat for awhile, and they talked about Jim. "He was a wonderful tenant," Liz said for about the hundredth time. "He was so neat and polite." Tom pressed for details, but there weren't many available. The women had never seen him with a friend, and they had little idea how he spent the long days and nights be-hind the closed door of his apartment. They hadn't noticed him using the pay phone at the end of the walkway. "About once a month, around the time his check came, he'd leave for a few days," Liz offered. "Don't know where he went to. Maybe Austin. There's a bus over by Fort Hood."

Tom was depressed by how little they could tell him. These kind women were the closest thing Jim had had to a family, yet he'd kept them at arm's length. He'd lived like an outlaw, a man in hiding. What was he hiding from?

Finally, Tom stood up to leave, and Liz walked outside with him. She surprised him with a tight hug. "You tell your mother we are praying for James," she said. "You tell her what a good boy he was."

At the police station, Tom spoke briefly with the two officers who had found Jim's body. They had little to say but were polite. "Ah," the baby-faced officer drawled, "Looked like natural causes"—as if there were anything natural about a fifty-three-year-old man dropping dead while he watched television.

Tom was ushered into the sheriff's office, where a burly man with sandy hair and a florid face sat with his scuffed cowboy boots propped up on his desk. A cowboy hat was tossed on a nearby table. The walls and shelves were filled with memorabilia and trinkets—a laminated wooden clock in the shape of Texas, an autographed football, a photo of the sheriff flanked by bodacious cheerleaders, a framed award from the Killeen Chamber of Commerce.

The sheriff eyed Tom with a suspicious once-over that made him sweat. Without a word he handed Tom a wallet and a bank book that had been taken from Jim's apartment. The wallet held a couple of dollars and some change. The bank book showed a balance of $62.

"That should do it," the sheriff said in an unfriendly way. Tom mumbled his thanks and got the hell out of there.

Tom flew home with the small bag containing Jim's medals, his wallet, and the address book, leaving Killeen with more questions than ever. Jim's body was shipped to Washington State, and we buried him a week later, on the eve of September 11, 2001.

TWO

———

AN ARMY
OF YOUTH

Plastic green army men littered the yards of our childhood. They stood sentry in the crooks of trees, they were entrenched in the blackberry bushes, they hid behind the hedges, they burrowed deep in the foxholes of the sandbox. There were hundreds of them, tiny three-inch warriors posed in battle-ready stillness— a rifle aimed, a bazooka positioned, a hand grenade in mid-throw, an arm raised. My brothers collected them by the bagful and used them to spin out their imaginary battles. The combat zone of our backyard was a wildly informal recreation of the European theater. Everyone was thrilled to refight a war with a victorious ending. There were Nazi army men, too, with miniature red swastikas painted on their gray uniforms. Defeat and destruction was their destiny.

In the safety of our peacetime world, war games were everyday and without consequence, something to do on long summer afternoons. Years after all the boyhood strategies had been determined and the battles had been won, we'd find a stray army man buried beneath our mother's fragrant rose bushes, or a tiny bazooka man forlorn and forgotten in a dusty corner of the basement.

I never knew a girl with battlefield dreams, including myself, but the landscape of boyhood was littered with toy guns and plastic soldiers. War games separated the boys from the girls, just as real war (in our generation, at least) would separate the men from the women.

We were raised in a family that revered military service. Our great-great grandfather had been a Union soldier during the Civil War. The walls of our living room were lined with the portraits of war—our grandfathers stern and unsmiling in World War I army uniforms, our father in his navy whites during World War II. The thundering chords of "Victory at Sea" frequently spilled from our father's scratchy record player. We were the children of the greatest generation, raised on a diet of war movies—*The Sands of Iwo Jima, Bridge on the River Kwai, Twelve O'Clock High, From Here to Eternity, Stalag 17, Pork Chop Hill*—our heroes cast in Hollywood. When the likes of John Wayne, Clark Gable, Gregory Peck, Errol Flynn, or William Holden marched or sailed into battle, we had no trouble believing it was for a noble and worthy cause. Our Hollywood heroes brought great panache to their many war-themed films, inspiring thousands upon thousands to follow in their glorious footsteps and serve their nation.

We were innocent receptacles for the great idea of the times— that war could be just and holy when waged against the forces of evil. Our guys, as depicted in the media, were good, brave, all-American boys, older versions of our sandlot players, who could always be relied upon to save the world when it needed it the most.

The nobility of war was inextricably linked with faith. In our Catholic school classrooms, the central parable of our religion was the fight between good and evil. As early as the first grade, the nuns taught us about the greatest battle of all time—the epic confrontation between Michael the Archangel and the devil Lucifer. We learned that Lucifer had once been an angel, even God's favorite angel. But he fell from grace when he challenged God's dominion. Michael, depicted in white garb as pure as snow, with wings that spanned the universe, wielded his sword with heroic force, sending the dark angels to hell.

"Children, imagine if Saint Michael had lost that battle," I remember our first grade teacher saying with breathless solemnity. "Where would we be now?"

Our eyes grew wide trying to imagine such darkness and despair, but we didn't really have to imagine it. Our religion textbooks were filled with pictures of fiery dungeons, their flames consuming the screaming demons. Thank God for Michael! Our gratitude to the world's first soldier was boundless and sincere, even as we were forced to acknowledge that the job was not complete. We still needed Michael to stand at the ready, and so we prayed every day:

Saint Michael the Archangel, defend us in battle.
Be our safeguard against the wickedness
    and snares of the devil.
Cast into hell Satan and all the evil spirits.

In Catholic schools of the 1950s and 1960s, we were indoctrinated not in the ways of peace, but in the ways of war. Small and innocent, we were called to be warriors in Christ's army, and although we couldn't quite understand what that meant, we marched around our classrooms singing the Christian battle song:

An army of youth,
Flying banners of truth,
We are fighting for Christ the Lord.
Heads lifted high,
Catholic action our cry,
And the cross our only sword.

War was like air—always there, a necessity of life and a form of salvation. Earth itself was a battlefield, with new enemies constantly on the horizon. For us, supplanting Nazism was Communism. Our indoctrination in the evils of Communism was carried out through the prism of faith. Communists were unbelievers whose mission was to force atheism on the masses. We heard apocryphal stories of small children banished to Siberia or even killed because they wanted to pray. (The subtext was always, "Would you suffer so bravely for Jesus?") These stories fit well with the equally heroic lives of the saints, especially the martyrs, who endured extreme torture and death to defend the faith—heroes like Saint Lawrence, a Spanish martyr in the third century, who was burned alive on a spit by a mob of unbelievers, and who is said to have responded to the taunts of his torturers by crying out, "Turn me over; I'm not done yet."

The perennial favorite was Joan of Arc, whose courage in battle gave her legitimacy in nonreligious circles as well. A World War II poster featured Saint Joan in full armor, dagger raised:

JOAN OF ARC SAVED FRANCE
WOMEN OF AMERICA
SAVE YOUR COUNTRY
BUY WAR SAVINGS STAMPS

It wasn't just the Catholic Church that preached the evils of Communism. In the 1950s, Billy Graham made it clear just what was at stake: "Either Communism must die or Christianity must die, because it is actually a battle between Christ and anti-Christ."

In other words, onward Christian soldiers. Better dead than Red.

═══

Seattle in the post–World War II era was a young city on the brink of greatness. Freeways, ferry systems, skyscrapers, and the iconic Space Needle were just around the bend. It was ready to become an urban center with small-town values. Clean streets, fresh air, and breathtaking vistas offered an idyllic lifestyle that larger, older cities could not match. A thriving seaport and burgeoning aerospace industry promised healthy employment opportunities. It was a period of boundless optimism.

That's not to say that all was so right with our world. Thinking back, I see more clearly what wasn't apparent then—that my father's war had taken its toll. My father was no longer alive to read Tom Brokaw's portrayal of his war years, or to hear himself described as a member of the greatest generation, but knowing Dad, he wouldn't have thought much of it. He was an unsentimental man who was proud of his military service, but rarely spoke of it in concrete terms. Sometimes he'd imply that it was pretty miserable, even downright terrifying, out on the open ocean, standing guard, alone and shivering through long nights, the sky as black as death, the enormous swells crashing over the bow potentially alive with enemy torpedoes. But he never lingered on those memories.

My father enlisted in the navy in 1940, right out of high school, the only child of our widowed grandmother. Neither of them ever suggested there was any pathos in their sacrifice. War was on the horizon by then, and everyone was shipping out. Dad set sail on the original USS *Kitty Hawk*, headed for the South Pacific. He spent years at sea, and participated in the Battle of Midway, while his mother worried back home. A yellowed, frayed *Seattle Times* newspaper article from that period contains an interview with my grandmother, who laments, "I haven't heard from him in almost two months. The last time he wrote he said: 'If for any reason you don't hear from me, remember, no news is good news.' But I still run out to meet the mailman so often he says he guesses he'll have to write me a letter himself."

Dad was a signalman, which meant he was often posted in the crow's nest high above the ship's platform, sending and receiving signals and acting as a lookout. From his lonely perch, he had plenty of time for reflection, and his letters home were vivid and poetic:

> I have my cot on the flying bridge, which is the highest part of the ship, and I have the honor of sleeping under a billion stars with the nice cool ocean breeze blowing. Sometimes I think this whole mess is merely a dream and when I awake in the morning I will find myself at home. But I'm not able to look around without being convinced of the reality of it all.

Later in the war, Dad was assigned to a minesweeper in the desolate hinterlands of the Aleutian Islands and Alaska, where the threat from Japan was constant. This was truly a no-man's-land—a place of soupy fog, bone-chilling cold, and fierce blizzards. The navy had an outpost on Kodiak Island. Locals like to refer to Kodiak as Alaska's Emerald Isle, but it's hard to credit the nickname from my father's World War II photos, which show a gray, isolated, rickety base, with grim sailors bundled heavily against the cold.

Perhaps an indication of my father's desolation was that for the first time in his life he turned to religion. Father Edgar Gallant (the first priest ordained in Alaska) ran a small mission church on the island, and my father befriended the tall, loquacious priest with a roaring laugh and burly frame. He was as un-churchlike as they come, and Dad, who never had much use for pompous displays of religiosity, was drawn to Father Gallant's style of Catholicism. He converted to the Catholic Church on

Kodiak Island and remained friends with Father Gallant until the priest died decades later. Dad used to tell us, "Father Gallant was a man's man."

Back home in Seattle, my father's relationship to the Great War was mostly silence. I don't recall hearing a single story of his service, and old navy buddies didn't drop by or hang out in our home reminiscing over a few beers. It never struck me as the least bit peculiar. Nearly everyone we knew was a veteran, and none of them ever talked about it either. When I began researching this book, I made it a point to ask friends and acquaintances about their fathers' service in World War II, and in every case I received the same answer: "He never talked about it."

To be sure, many of the World War II veterans that filled VFW halls talked of nothing else, but overwhelmingly, the most striking characteristic of that generation was its silence. The journalist Tom Mathews captured this mood in his beautifully written book, *Our Fathers' War*. "My father hated war stories," Mathews writes. "He was a soldier with a code, a brave man who wouldn't talk about World War II."

Publicly stoic and privately haunted, these veterans nevertheless saw the value of that code. My father's generation was rigorous about never showing weakness on the home front, never shedding tears, never letting down its guard. Seen through their eyes, it was impossible to imagine an unjust war, but they were unable to tell their stories.

There was always another war, a new evil. There was always a fresh challenge against which our rockets red glare would again light the darkness. In *War Is a Force That Gives Us Meaning*, journalist Chris Hedges writes: "War makes the world understandable, a black and white tableau of them and us. All bow before the supreme effort. We are one. Most of us willingly accept war as

long as we can fold it into a belief system that paints the ensuing
suffering as necessary for a higher good, for human beings seek
not only happiness but also meaning."

It is this meaning, found in the popular narratives of war, that
is so seductive. We write an epic script that fits the need for
meaning, blurring the actual details with metaphor. We ride Saint
Michael's mighty wings into battle with a moral clarity that defies
the messy truth. This righteousness allows us as a nation to look
at the smoldering landscapes of Hiroshima and My Lai and Baghdad and proclaim, "It is good."

The history of humanity may be soaked in the blood of war,
but killing another human being is not a natural instinct. It relies
on an explosive cocktail of great myth and personal adrenaline.
The detonator in every war is the dehumanization of the enemy.
To be successful on the battlefield, a soldier must be able to look
another soldier in the eye and not only think, "This is my enemy,"
but also, "This man is not like me. He is a barbarian. He has no
soul. His death is of no consequence." In Nazi Germany, the concept of *Lebensunwertes Leben*—literally, "life unworthy of life"—
was essential to achieve national cooperation in the extermination
of the Jews. In our era, this transposition of evil on the enemy has
been more easily accomplished when the enemy looks physically
different from us. The slurs of recent wars—the *chinks*, *nips*, and
gooks of Asian conflicts, or the *towel heads*, *sand niggers*, and *Hajis*
in the Middle East—intensify that emotional distance. General
William Westmoreland once referred to the Vietnamese as "ter-
mites," and this dehumanization was undoubtedly a contributing
factor in one of the most shameful incidents of the Vietnam War,
the My Lai massacre. During his court-martial testimony, Lieu-
tenant William Calley explained the slaughter of an entire village
of Vietnamese men, women, and children with these words: "I
was ordered to go in there and destroy the enemy. That was my

job on that day. That was the mission I was given. I did not sit down and think in terms of men, women, and children. They were all classified the same, and that was the classification that we dealt with, just as enemy soldiers."

The dehumanization of the enemy, and by extension the race to which it belongs, has been made easier by the philosophy of American exceptionalism. Exceptionalism holds us apart from others by virtue of our unique heritage and values. American exceptionalism is inherently narcissistic. It is also dangerous when power is placed in the hands of the true believers.

If you look closely, you can see the buildup to war in rhetoric long before the first shot is fired. Rhetoric is the grease that primes the public will. The domino theory, which became the central premise behind the Vietnam War, had its origins in the Eisenhower administration, many years before a single soldier was committed to fight. Wars, as they say, are not started by soldiers, but by politicians.

These images were effective and easy to swallow when the battlefront was far away. Ironically, the domino theory predated and was similar to the rallying cry of our current engagements—"Fight them over there so we don't have to fight them over here." One proponent of the Vietnam War declared, "It is far better to fight in Vietnam—on China's doorstep—than fight some years hence in Hawaii, on our own frontiers."

And so, off we marched to replicate our fathers' heroism and save the world once again. But things didn't turn out so well. Our grandiosity and self-reverence took a beating with the Vietnam War. Here, at last, was a more ambiguous battleground. Coupled with a cultural time bomb ready to explode in the late sixties, it rocked our sense of ourselves and gave rise to doubts about our national code of honor.

In the aftermath of Vietnam, there was a sense that we would have to find better ways to solve global problems—that the complexity of foreign cultures and conflicts could not be settled by obliterating the enemy. One clear legacy of the Vietnam War was an energized peace movement that even infiltrated the ranks of the military.

When the Vietnam War ended badly, the nation began to engage in a healthy conversation about the costs versus benefits of committing our soldiers to vast, uncertain enterprises. For the next sixteen years we avoided all-out war. Had the Gulf War lasted longer and produced more casualties, there is no question that the outcry would have been huge. Instead, the United States began the twenty-first century with most of the population in a peacetime frame of mind, even as busy bands of neocons began laying the groundwork for future engagements.

In the years before September 11, the clarion call of our fathers' war began to sound, as if the culture itself were sensing the need to prepare us for a battle that had not yet started. Vietnam had shaken our faith. The Gulf War had left us uneasy. The embers of collective intention were smoldering and threatening to die.

If the nation could be transported once more to that mythical time, perhaps we could be great again, flex our muscles as a super power.

This was achieved first with Steven Spielberg's movie *Saving Private Ryan*, the second highest grossing movie of 1998, which returned the archetypal soldier hero to the screens. Although unsparing in its brutal depictions, it was also sodden with old-world sentimentality. *Ryan* recreated the Good War through the eyes of our hero, played by that icon of Americana, Tom Hanks. The simple chapter and verse of war was restored: good will conquer evil.

The glorification of World War II became a drum roll and then a roar with Tom Brokaw's 1998 bestseller, *The Greatest Gen-*

eration. Brokaw painted a sharp contrast between the World War II generation and its children. Our fathers, he wrote, "answered the call to help save the world from the two most powerful and ruthless military machines ever assembled, instruments of conquest in the hands of fascist maniacs. They faced great odds and a late start, but they did not protest . . ." And, Brokaw adds, when the war was over, our fathers "immediately began the task of rebuilding their lives and the world they wanted."

In *The Greatest Generation*, Brokaw seemed to lead the nation in a chiding chorus, saying, in effect, *Look at these men and women who came through the Great Depression and World War II, yet landed on their feet and shaped the future of our country. Why can't you be more like them?*

Brokaw's book had an almost hypnotic effect on the public, as historian Doris Kearns Goodwin notes, without disguising her approval. "The stories Brokaw tells are so powerful that a spell is cast upon the reader," she writes. And that seemed to be true. Efforts to raise the possibility that greatness might also be found in peace were met with contempt, as the yammerings of the unpatriotic.

The events of 9/11 presented the ideal opportunity to match rhetoric with action. Any lingering notion that war was not the answer was buried in the rubble. Evil had swept over us with the power of Lucifer himself, and suddenly the military training camps were filling up again, with small town would-be heroes ready to fight.

In the beginning, the war effort was fueled by righteous indignation, and then by a fervor for proselytizing reminiscent of the epic Crusades. We would bring freedom to the world. It's too bad that the old warrior of morality, Bishop Fulton J. Sheen, was no longer around to set us straight. Bishop Sheen was a feature on 1950s television screens, a man of great intellect who could reach the common man with his clear thinking and wry humor.

My parents watched his program *religiously* every Friday night. Bishop Sheen was a vehement and articulate foe of Communism, although he later opposed the war in Vietnam. But in his writings a moral clarity shines through, so applicable to our vision of war today:

> One of the greatest disasters that happened to modern civilization was for democracy to inscribe "liberty" on its banners instead of "justice." Because "liberty" was considered the ideal it was not long until some men interpreted it as meaning "freedom from justice"; then when religion and decent government attempted to bring them back to justice, organizing into "freedom groups" they protested that their constitutional and natural rights were being violated. The industrial and social injustice of our era is the tragic aftermath of democracy's overemphasis on freedom as the "right to do whatever you please." No, freedom means the right to do what you ought, and ought implies law, and law implies justice, and justice implies God. So, too, in war, a nation that fights for freedom divorced from justice has no right to war, because it does not know why it wants to be free, or why it wants anyone else to be free.

Our march to war in Afghanistan, and later, Iraq, was made on the flag of freedom, on President Bush's promise to bring democracy to the Middle East. At the time, it was a call that resonated. Edward W. Wood Jr., a World War II veteran and the author of *Worshipping the Myths of World War II: Reflections on America's Dedication to War*, could see it all coming. "The story told in the mainline media explains why it was so easy for America to accept the idea of a 'war on terror,'" he writes. "Once again, we would storm the beaches of Normandy . . . bomb the people of Japan. Our policies of preemption, our war with Iraq, are rooted in a war now sixty years past."

Watching the newscasts on March 21, 2003, the night we bombed Baghdad, you could hear the thrill in the anchors' voices, the raw excitement, the joy of shock and awe. Wolf Blitzer's eyes were alight as he reported that in his thirty years of reporting, he had never seen anything on the scale of America's attack on the Iraqi capital.

The commander in chief's bullish rhetoric—defeating evil, chasing Osama Bin Laden to the gates of hell—set the tone for our engagement and inspired the young to follow. Bush was the Pied Piper for a new generation of fighting men and women.

Jerry Lembcke, a sociology professor at Holy Cross College in Worcester, Massachusetts, who served as an army chaplain in Vietnam, observed, "Over the years the thought congealed for me: 'War is hell' isn't working as an antiwar slogan. Worse, I feared, the horror of war might be a kind of catnip for young men. The worse we make it sound and look, the more irresistible it is. Maybe it's the Calvinism engrained in American culture that calls us to duty—the greater the risk, the greater the glory. No cost, no benefit."

But when the promised victory was slow in coming, the public began to lose its appetite for the Iraq War. That's when the people pulling the propaganda strings took action. They'd learned their lesson from Vietnam: when the legitimacy of a war is in doubt, find a hero and tell a story. And so, in the early days of the Iraq War, we were supplied with two.

Jessica Lynch arrived just when we needed her, when the confidence of the nation was beginning to waver over a conflict that was bogging down after its initial, glorious surge. Lynch's story seemed too good to be true—wonderful and terrible all at once—and it succeeded in stirring the embers of our patriotic fire. Lynch was a nineteen-year-old supply clerk from Palestine, West Virginia, serving with the U.S. Army's 507th Ordinance Maintenance Company. When a convoy in which she was riding took a wrong turn and was ambushed near Nasiriya, it was said that Lynch bravely fought off the enemy, like a modern day Annie Oakley, gun blazing, as her comrades were slaughtered around her. Initial news reports told of how she fired and fired until she no longer could. "She was fighting to the death," a U.S. official told reporters. "She did not want to be taken alive." Severely wounded, with multiple bullet and stab wounds, our brave, blonde heroine was captured by Iraqi forces and held prisoner for eight days at a local hospital. There were rumors of a possible sexual assault—journalistic red meat for the masses. And then, miraculously, she was rescued in a midnight raid, conveniently captured on film, by an elite squad of Army Rangers and Navy SEALs, who stormed the hospital and whisked her away to a waiting helicopter. It was said that they came under enemy fire.

Almost immediately, the credibility of the account began to take on water, sinking with the weight of contrary evidence.

According to staff at the hospital, Iraqi soldiers had fled days earlier, and the military knew it. There was no resistance. And although Lynch suffered a broken arm and a broken thigh, there were no bullet or stab wounds. Lynch herself crushed the best part of the story—that she went down, gun blazing, in defense of her comrades. Actually, Lynch remembered nothing of the incident. The story we were fed was mostly fiction, as Lynch herself acknowledged in a 2007 congressional hearing.

The hyperbole surrounding the tale might be deemed harmless—the kind of war story worthy of a culture that produced *Saving Private Ryan*. More damaging was the second iconic story of the war involving Pat Tillman. When Tillman left behind a $3.6 million contract with the NFL and a beautiful new wife to join the army after the attacks of September 11, his story became one more example that this was a war worth fighting. Young, handsome, strong, and glowingly patriotic, Tillman was an instant media hero before he ever stepped foot in Afghanistan. When he died there on April 22, 2004, the army told his family he had been killed by enemy fire after courageously charging up a hill to protect his fellow rangers. The army awarded Tillman a Silver Star for "gallantry in action against an armed enemy."

From the start, Mary Tillman, Pat's mother—arguably the person most likely to take comfort in the story—felt that it didn't ring true, and said so. "It sounded kind of like a John Wayne movie," she said doubtfully. A month after Tillman's death, the truth came out. He had been killed by his own men.

So-called friendly fire is inevitable in the fog of war, but its stigma is enormous. That is why we rarely hear that an estimated 21 percent of Word War II casualties and 39 percent of Vietnam War casualties occurred this way. The estimate in Iraq currently hovers around 41 percent.

The specter of friendly fire contradicts the purity of the mission, even as it crushes the psyches of the soldiers involved. It is a terrible wake-up call for those who want to glorify the necessity of war. Much of the public anger surrounding Pat Tillman's story was directed not at those who told the initial lie but at those who reported the truth. It was a serious blow to morale. "Why did they have to ruin it?" many asked plaintively. He was our warrior prince, and then he was just another victim.

The glorification of prior generations of warriors and the airbrushed treatment of today's soldiers undercuts efforts to seriously evaluate the service-related realities of the current generation, especially the tens of thousands of returning soldiers who suffer from post-traumatic stress disorder. For soldiers, sailors, airmen, and marines, life is never the way it appears on our screens. The rhetoric is a hollow tribute to the actual experience.

The soldiers who do the fighting are no more real to us than the green army men who fought in the shrubbery of our backyards so long ago. The vast majority of us cannot identify with them or know them. And when we're done playing with them, we leave them under the bushes, forgotten.

Today, the inequality of the costs of war has become too great to ignore. An army of youth makes the sacrifices, and the rest of us enjoy a gentle oblivion. As our leaders speak of chasing terrorists to the gates of hell, the soldiers returning home see it differently. Many of them face a bitter truth: the gates of hell are right here, in our midst.

THREE

JIM'S WAR

1966

"JIM WAS THE bravest boy I ever knew," my mother told me recently. I smiled in agreement, remembering some of his childhood antics. I wondered if my brother was feeling brave that November day in 1966 as his 707 banked over the Pacific Ocean and began its descent into Bien Hoa Air Base. Was he feeling brave as he clamored down the airliner's stairs to the tarmac and fell into the searing embrace of the heat and humidity, filling his lungs for the first time with the pungent mix of decay and burning jet fuel exhaust that welcomed him to Vietnam? Was he feeling brave as he faced the most compelling test of his young life?

In the four months since enlisting in the army, had Jim made the transition from boy to man? For most seventeen-year-olds, courage was measured by lesser challenges—a football skirmish with a daring plunge into a yielding wall of flesh, or summoning the nerve to ask a pretty girl on a date. Guts were exhibited in schoolyard antics, or hiding out with a couple of fellow outlaws, boldly chugging stolen whiskey.

But war was a different matter. War was a man's place, and even if Jim and his fellow soldiers were mere boys in any other context, their very survival—never mind success—required that they now behave as men.

There was no way for any of us to know what Jim experienced as he began his first tour of duty. He was a young novice soldier in the first posting of what became a long military career. Perhaps he had already decided this was his life, that he had found his calling.

Jim had left our sheltered household, where curfews were still enforced and attendance at Sunday Mass was mandatory. It was a violence-free zone, a peacetime haven that our parents worked hard to maintain. The only gun in the house was an old, inoperable rifle that had once belonged to our grandfather. Dad kept the dusty antique under his bed—just in case an empty threat were ever needed.

Jim's place in that world was as the second son in a brood of nine, although when he left for Vietnam, it was still a brood of eight. Our youngest sister, Joanne, was born while Jim was in Vietnam. The spread of our ages spanned more than two decades and two distinct eras. The three eldest—Greg, born in 1946, Jim, in 1948, and I, in 1950—were the original baby boomers, while the three youngest—John, born in 1962, Margy in 1964, and Joanne, in 1967—were on the cusp of Generation X. The remaining three landed in the middle—Paul, in 1952, Tom, in 1955, and Mary, in 1957.

Greg, Jim, and I were the vanguard in this growing family, bonded in early childhood through our shared adventures—two redheaded boys and a little blonde girl, set loose upon a neighborhood bursting with kids.

Of all the siblings, only Greg and I knew Jim well as children, and my earliest memories of him were of a devilishly charismatic little boy, forever egging me on to be more adventuresome than I could ever be on my own. Mom's characterization of his bravery is accurate. From an early age, Jim lived life as though each day were a dare. He would climb higher in a tree, ride farther on his bike, stand longer on the railroad tracks as they vibrated with the approach of a speeding train. He excelled at sports because he was always willing to take risks.

Jim was the rebel in our culture of obedience. He'd get ideas into his head that were preposterous, but exciting, and more often than not I would trail along. On one occasion, he happened to find a bucket of red paint, and convinced me that it would be fun to paint a neighbor's white fence. He was six, I was four. Another time, he figured out a way to unlock the kitchen window of our next-door neighbors' house while they were on vacation, and invited me to crawl in behind him and watch television in their dark living room.

Jim's streak of lawlessness got him into a lot of trouble, but for some reason I was never blamed, and I was happy to be seen as an innocent bystander, whether it was true or not.

Jim's redeeming quality was his charm. There was a sweetness about him, even at his naughtiest, that belied any wrong intentions. Jim struggled in school, but looking at his old report cards, I can see that the nuns were charmed as well. They were full of warnings, but also of absolution. Everyone was certain that Jim would straighten out eventually. And Jim did try, in his own way, to walk the straight and narrow. Along with Greg, he was an altar boy, had a paper route, and played organized sports. But he was restless. He wanted something else. Something more.

With the benefit of hindsight, I suspect that Jim had a learning disability that made school especially challenging for him. If he were a child today, he might have been diagnosed with dyslexia; he was always getting his words mixed up. ADHD might have explained his willful personality. But at the time, the solution was always to "try harder" and "be good." Our parents and teachers pushed and prodded him mercilessly, as if by sheer force of their will he would buckle down, but their efforts had the opposite effect. They only reinforced his rebelliousness.

Jim was the poster boy for the curse of the second-born child. He was sandwiched as the filling between smart-as-a-whip Greg, the first son, and me, the adored first daughter. Imagine the pickle Jim found himself in. He could never be as smart or as good as his older brother, or as sweet and adorable as his little sister.

Jim was intent on carving out his own identity, to show the world he was special in his own right. If he couldn't be the smartest or the most adored, he'd be something else. Although our parents tried very hard to give equal measures of love and encouragement to all of their children, Jim never felt loved enough. He always craved more. As he got older, his troubles increased, and he began to grow apart from the clan. The more our mother tried to embrace him, the more he withdrew. Our parents, busy with the demands of their large family, weren't able to give him the extra attention he required. Even if they'd had the inclination or knowledge to seek professional help for him, they'd have had a hard time paying for it.

Antisocial behavior and charm are a volatile combination, and as we grew up, Jim became an intimidating presence around our neighborhood.

He got into fights over nothing—a lot of them. If you looked at him wrong, he'd start a fight. That's the way he was. When a couple of kids walloped us in a snowball fight, he beat them up. Our younger siblings looked up to Jim because he was the coolest person they knew, with his Brylcreemed hair and swagger. But they also learned to be wary of him, and to be afraid of his moods, which could change from loving to pissed off with the speed of lightning.

We didn't tiptoe around Jim; we just avoided poking at him like family members do with one another. It wasn't worth it. He was too easily angered. Even the little ones knew that.

Jim's enlistment in the United States Army at such a young age was not a grand patriotic moment. It was an alternative form of incarceration. When Jim got into a scrape with the law—not his first—Dad sided with a local judge who recommended that he join the army to avoid jail.

"Straighten him out. Make a man of him."

It wasn't so unusual at that time for troubled boys to enter the army directly from the courthouse. I've heard their stories—the petty larcenists, the amateur arsonists, the juvenile delinquents—who caught a "break" from kindly old judges. This may seem archaic and even shocking in a modern context, but I've learned that it still goes on, especially in small towns. (A shrinking pool of applicants has led the army to lower recruitment standards that were elevated for the volunteer forces, making this arrangement even more likely today.)

In the 1960s, it was considered a positive trade-off. Our parents, like so many others at the time, viewed military service as a character-building experience, and they saw the judge's suggestion as a brilliant solution for their trouble-prone boy. Jim was happy to oblige. He was glad to be rescued from the tedium of the classroom; tired of being the one in the family who was always considered a screwup. Perhaps he hoped to find a way to make everyone proud of him, after all.

But on the gray April morning when we gathered to watch him leave, it didn't feel like much of a hero's send-off.

As Dad packed Jim's duffel bag in the trunk of the car, the rest of us stood around in the chilly spring drizzle, bunched together, watching with wide eyes. We were a bit in awe, especially the younger ones.

"Can I go? Can I go?" three-year-old John begged, tugging at Dad's pant leg. Dad shook his head no. He was quiet that morning, his mouth cut in a grim line. Mom was teary-eyed. Jim gave her a quick hug, grinned at the bunched gaggle of kids, hopped into the car, and he and Dad pulled out of the driveway. Twenty years after he'd folded his navy uniform into a cedar chest, Dad was driving his second son to the bus station, not with feelings of pride, but with a sigh of relief mixed with a gnawing concern. Would he be all right? Could he take it? Dim memories of his own first days as a navy recruit flickered through Dad's mind.

In two days Jim would begin his basic training at Fort Ord in California. He'd never been outside Washington State, and the trip down the Pacific coastline was his first taste of independence. No more parents, no more books, no more teachers' dirty looks. Common sense should have told him that he would be facing something far worse, but he didn't see it that way. He was excited. Basic training seemed like an intense version of summer camp to Jim, something our large family had never been able to afford. He looked forward to the physical challenges, the mock battles, the opportunity to fire guns and throw hand grenades. For once in his life, he was entering an arena where he felt he could excel.

During the Vietnam War era, Ford Ord was the major training center for the United States Army on the West Coast. More than half a million soldiers were churned out of its boot camp grinder. Its pedigree was legendary. Clark Gable, Clint Eastwood, and Elvis Presley all did their basic training there. The cast of *Combat!*, a popular television show in the sixties, had also "trained" there.

Fort Ord was physically immense, a jarring note in the otherwise lush, serene landscape of Monterey Bay, California, one of the most beautiful areas of the country. The Pacific Ocean was a short drive away, and the bracing tang of sea air was carried inland on the wind.

By contrast, Fort Ord was a vast utilitarian complex—gray, noisy, busy, and ugly. It was a small city with rows of barracks, administration buildings, mess halls, latrines, training centers, weapons ranges, and acres and acres of open grasslands and hilly woods dedicated to simulating various battle conditions.

In 1966, the Vietnam War had already ratcheted up; 350,000 troops would be on the ground in Southeast Asia by year's end. The selective service system was in full force, so a good 25 percent of the troops coming in were draftees. Jim's army transport from the San Francisco bus station was crowded with recruits. They were all nervous and excited, but not all of them were glad to be going. Already there was a palpable difference between the volunteers and the draftees.

But the boys on the bus had one thing in common: they were all very young, the signs of puberty barely fading from their pimpled faces.

How, exactly, does one go from being a seventeen-year-old boy in a prom tuxedo with a boutonniere and a silly grin to a lean, mean killing machine? How does the transformation occur? How do you make someone ready and able to kill, and do it in the brief months of basic training? The formula rests on a combination of brainwashing and brutality, most effective on the malleable young. The objective of boot camp is to sublimate individuality to the greater good of the unit, break down resistance to authority, eliminate moral doubts, and maximize and hone aggressive tendencies.

Every new recruit had heard boot-camp horror stories of screaming pit-bull drill sergeants, harsh punishments for the merest infractions, and spirit-crushing humiliations. Were the rumors true?

An army recruitment video from the 1960s, set at Fort Ord and designed to ease the fears of new recruits and reassure their worried parents, presents an entirely different view. The video strains credulity with its soft-spoken commander and smiling, compassionate drill sergeants describing a kinder, gentler army, where recruits are treated like gentlemen, and discipline is meted out with less force than you'd find in a Catholic school classroom. The trainees interviewed for the video smile into the camera, saying things like, "It's not that hard," and, "It's just like a football game."

The film would probably make most boot-camp veterans howl with laughter. The truth is, you don't unlock the soul of a warrior by nurturing him in an environment of human kindness and respect. This version certainly doesn't square with the stories I heard from veterans. The memories of those who served in the army or marines are more in line with the depictions in films such as Stanley Kubrick's *Full Metal Jacket* or David Rabe's play *The Basic Training of Pavlo Hummel*, which had dark and terrifying undertones.

According to a study conducted by Brandon Johnson and Robert A. Goldberg of the University of Utah, abuse of recruits was a significant element of the United States Armed Forces basic training in the Vietnam War era. Their conclusion was based on oral histories and memoirs of army and marine recruits. While the army's training regimen was regarded as less brutal than that of the marines, the report reveals details of physical humiliation, stress, and experiences that left a permanent mark on trainees. "Psychological abuse and intimidation were key techniques by which trainees extended control over recruits," the study concluded. "In many cases it was the drill instructor's psychological abuse tactics that most induced new soldiers to embrace passivity and conformity."

The process began the minute recruits stepped off the bus into the care of screaming drill sergeants who called them "maggots" and "motherfuckers." The obligatory hair shaving was the first assault to individual identity, more a symbolic shearing of the civilian self than a military necessity.

There was also an elemental crudeness to basic training, a sexualization of the experience meant to shock the boys—many of them virgins—into becoming men. There are reports of trainees being made to run with rifles in one hand and their penises in the other, chanting, "This is my rifle, this is my gun, one is for fighting, one is for fun." To be a man, you had to have both a penis and a gun, and be able to "fire" both.

The task of basic training was to turn individuals into part of a whole, a cohesive unit that would follow orders without hesitation. They would know how to muster; how to advance; how to carry, fire, and clean their weapons; and how to behave as members of a military company. This required a lot of repetitive, boring training, both physical and mental, best accomplished in a group setting.

The cornerstone of unit discipline and cohesion was the drill. Marching and chanting, sometimes for hours on end, built a sense of company attunement. Chants were essential to the marches. They were known as Jodie calls. "Jodie" was a fictional civilian slacker back at home who stole your girlfriend, took your job, drank your beer, and lived the high life while you were at war. A common Jodie call went like this:

> *Ain't no use in going home;*
> *Jodie's got your girl and gone.*
> *Ain't no use in feeling blue;*
> *Jodie's got your sister, too.*
> *Ain't no use in lookin' back;*
> *Jodie's got your Cadillac . . .*

At times the Jodie calls had a more sinister intent because, after all, the real enemy was "over there"—the faceless, dehumanized Vietnamese. The Vietcong. The VC. Charlie.

I wanna go to Vietnam;
I wanna kill a Vietcong.
With a knife or with a gun;
Either way will be good fun.
Stomp 'em, beat 'em,
Kick 'em in the ass.
Hide their bodies in the grass.

Jim thrived in basic training. It fulfilled his need to belong, and he took to the physical challenges with a skill and enthusiasm that had been untapped in his civilian life. He discovered that he was an excellent marksman, and he proved fearless in live grenade training. Within the first month, Jim was singled out as one of the outstanding recruits, and he experienced the unfamiliar feeling of both belonging and pride in self. By the time Jim finished basic training, he had been transformed into a soldier.

Military training was divided into two parts. Basic was just that—the rudimentary skills all soldiers need to function as part of a military unit. The next stage was Advanced Individual Training, or AIT, an additional eight weeks of specialized training. That's when soldiers received their Military Occupational Specialty (MOS), and were then assigned to the post that would train and qualify them.

Many of the raw recruits were assigned to the infantry, but Jim was given a specialization. He was sent to Fort Leonard Wood, Missouri, the army's training center for combat engineers. It was a miserable posting. Jim wrote home:

It's so hot and buggy here, you wouldn't believe it. We call it
Fort Lost in the Woods, Misery. Our barracks are metal sheds,
and you never stop sweating. But the work is interesting. Today
I learned how to detonate a mine.

At that point in the war there was a desperate need for combat engineers, sometimes called pioneers, because they were the
first ones into a combat zone.

A pioneer who served in Vietnam once described it this way:

The pioneer's thankless job in Vietnam was to rappel down
ropes from helicopters while under enemy fire, into thick jungle, clear mines and booby traps, blast landing zones with high
explosives, kill all the enemy here and there, and set up
perimeter defenses so the infantry could land.

That was just the half of it. Combat engineers were required
to play a multitude of roles, including fighting alongside the infantry when it became necessary, and clearing vast swaths of jungle using high explosives, heavy equipment, and machetes.

The irony of the old tune, "You're in the army now, you're
not behind a plow," was not lost on the engineers, who drove the
massive Rome plows that made combat missions possible in
Vietnam.

After Jim completed his training and received his assignment to Vietnam, he encountered the first demoralizing reality of
this war. Unlike World War II and the Korean War, when entire
companies were shipped out and remained together for the duration of their service, the Vietnam War operated on a system of
individual replacements. Every soldier's tour of duty in Vietnam
was twelve months. When his time was up, he was replaced by
another individual. This strict adherence to a precise length of

service was designed to boost morale; everyone knew exactly when they'd be going home. But the goal, while admirable, inadvertently created another kind of stress—feelings of loneliness and isolation that were a shocking change for soldiers who had formed some of the closest relationships of their lives during training. Due to the manner in which the army was now assigning its troops, chances were high that soldiers would never see their buddies again.

Instead, they would be dropped one by one into already formed units, always the outsider, akin to being the new kid in school. This was a blow to unit integrity, never mind individual morale. It was as though troop allocations had been designed to foster alienation and a sense of social isolation.

Combat engineers, in particular, were relegated to individual service. Moved around in ones and twos from battalion to battalion, brigade to brigade, division to division, company to company, they filled a myriad number of functions. Engineers were desperately needed everywhere—they plowed the earth, cleared the dense jungles, set up communication stations. And so, before he ever stepped foot in Vietnam, Jim learned his first bitter lesson: don't get overly attached to your buddies.

As many veterans have recounted, the flight to Vietnam on a civilian 707 was an incongruous experience. It might have been a vacation jaunt, with pretty, smiling stewardesses, in-flight movies, and easy-listening music. The only thing missing was the alcohol. Most new soldiers were below the drinking age, and in any case it was probably determined that a planeload of boozed-up replacements would not be a welcome sight on the ground in Vietnam.

Jim's first act after alighting on Asian soil might have been to run. It wasn't uncommon for transport planes to be fired upon, and many soldiers spent their first moments on the ground running for cover past the rows of body bags that would replace their spanking new duffels in the luggage hold. The first blast of choking hot air surely would have greeted Jim as a shock. Raised in the cool, rainy Pacific Northwest, he had struggled with the heat and humidity in Missouri; this was Missouri squared.

The rainy season in Vietnam was just ending when Jim arrived, and that was both a blessing and a curse. During the rainy season, which lasted roughly from April to October, soldiers were always cold and wet, slogging through mud by day and shivering in the surprising chill of long nights. The dry season, initially a relief, brought its own torments—unforgiving temperatures, hovering around the 100-degree mark at midday, sapping strength and clarity, and swarms of red ants that plucked at the skin like miniature shrapnel bursts.

What were Jim's expectations as he stepped off the plane? These were still early days for the war—nine years from its conclusion. I imagine that Jim had at least two expectations at the time. First, that the enemy was no competition for the American forces. President Johnson himself referred to Vietnam as a "ragged-ass little fourth rate country," and his characterization had been repeatedly reinforced during training. Jim's second expectation was undoubtedly that the army was a welcome presence for the South Vietnamese population. Eerily predating a future conflict, the myth still circulated that Americans would be "greeted as liberators." There was little understanding of the historical factors that brought them there. That course had been skipped in boot camp.

Jungle warfare among an indigenous population, indistinguishable from the enemy, was the greatest stress of the Vietnam War. The mission was presented as straightforward: save the South Vietnamese from the evil Vietcong. But the civilians didn't seem to want to be saved. Many were in collaboration with the

enemy, out of ideology or fear or self-interest, and American soldiers quickly learned the first rule of combat: trust no one. A
child on the road, a mother with a baby, a worker in the rice paddies or rubber plantations—any one of them might harbor a
weapon or explosive. Many American soldiers would come to
despise the people they were committed to rescue. The distinc-
tion between friend and foe disappeared. They were all the
same—*gooks*, *slopes*, *dinks*—and not quite human.

A similar mission confusion would occur decades later in
Iraq. The insurgents setting roadside bombs and ambushing con-
voys were identical to friendly citizens, and could only be conquered by fostering distrust of the entire population; thus, they
all came to be viewed as *towelheads*, *sand niggers*, and *dune coons*.
In this environment, collateral damage (the sanitized term for
killing innocent civilians) was inevitable. Indigenous populations
always suffer vastly more casualties than the military on either
side of a conflict. While more than 58,000 American troops lost
their lives in Vietnam, a price deemed far too high to pay, the toll
on the South Vietnamese population was staggering. Three million killed, three million wounded, and fifteen million refugees.

Many veterans who served in Vietnam have spoken about the
grave disappointment and confusion they felt when they learned
the truth of the populace's ambivalence about their presence. As
Bob Hope joked in a USO show in 1967, "I have good news. The
country is behind you 50 percent."

Jim was assigned to the First Engineer Battalion whose task
was to support the First Infantry Division. The First Engineers
were the oldest in the nation, dating back to the Civil War. The
battalion earned its moniker, "Diehard Engineers," in the North
Africa campaign of World War II. During that conflict, the battalion was fighting as infantry, and it was so unyielding on the
battlefield that a captured German officer said it was hard to kill;
it "died hard."

A battalion song captures its grit and spirit:

THE DIEHARD ENGINEER
(To the tune of "Clementine")

In a dozer, on a Rome Plow,
Clearing jungle without fear,
Is the best man in the Army,
He's a Diehard Engineer.
When there's mining, when there's LZ's,
And there's Charlie all about,
It's First Engineer assistance,
That will always bail you out.
On a highway at the bridge site,
VC watching from the trees,
There the Diehard Engineer stands,
Muddy water to his knees.

When Jim reached base camp, he would have encountered the grizzled band of engineers who'd already seen it all, done it all. Jim was, in the parlance of the time, a FNG—fucking new guy. The war-weary short-timers both welcomed and feared FNGs. On the one hand, they were a vision—the fresh meat of the war that would bring them closer to a flight home. On the other hand, when you were trusting your life to the men around you, it was a bit unsettling to see these awestruck, scared, excited newcomers, with pressed uniforms and shoes still shined, only twenty-odd hours away from their last trip to McDonald's. So the initial welcome was frosty. You had to earn the respect of your company. Fair enough.

The engineers had a twofold mission in Vietnam that was also a contradiction—build and destroy. One of the great ironies of the war was that the engineers were engaged in massive building projects even as they engaged in massive destruction. An estimated

11 million gallons of Agent Orange and 400,000 tons of napalm ravaged coconut groves, rubber plantations, and rice paddies, obliterating the economy and decimating crops that might have fed 2 million people. Six million tons of bombs destroyed thousands of hamlets and millions of acres of forest. At the same time, the army engineers were tasked to assist in the development of an emerging nation, building highways and bridges, developing ports, installing plumbing and sewage systems, and building schools and hospitals.

Commenting on the civic action program, Brigadier General Harold R. Parfitt reported in 1969:

> The special circumstances in this war have permitted the engineers to do a lot more work than ever before in nation building. Construction of major road networks, opening of secondary roads; a multiplicity of revolutionary development; all have contributed to improving the nation in such a way that the average citizen could see and appreciate what was being done by U.S. troops to improve his lot. To many people reared in poverty and misery, this was as meaningful as or more so than our efforts to prevent communist domination of their country.

It was a schizophrenic mission.

The way he saw it, Jim was in the destruction business. Once, when asked about his function in Vietnam that year, he replied simply, "I blew things up." But, of course, his mission was much greater.

Jim was stationed with Company C—Charlie Company—in Lai Khe, a Vietnamese village and American base camp set amid rubber plantations thirty-two miles north of Saigon. According to one of his former company mates, they were involved in sweeping for mines, cutting LZs (landing zones) for helicopter landings, and clearing and detonating the maze of tunnels that harbored thousands of the enemy—the work of the famed "tunnel rats."

One vet laughed when he recalled that sometimes the infantrymen referred to them as REMFs—Rear Echelon Mother Fuckers—but he wasn't really insulted because the nickname was so ludicrous. "We did it all," he said proudly. "On a daily basis we were called on to fight, whether on guard duty after a brutal workday, or when snipers hit, which they did constantly. If you want to know what it was like, imagine being on a construction site, building a bridge or a building, and having people trying to pick you off the whole time."

During this period, the military was gearing up for Operation Junction City, named for Junction City, Kansas, the home of the operation's commanding officer. It would be the largest military offensive of the war, involving thirty thousand American troops, a massive search-and-destroy mission in the Iron Triangle north of Saigon, believed to be the headquarters of the Vietcong.

The engineers' task was to clear mines and shore up Route 13, known as Thunder Road, the main supply route, running from Saigon to the Cambodian border. The road was surrounded by large rubber plantations that fell away into dense jungles. Vietnam's rubber trees were one of its most lucrative resources, left behind by the French when they departed in the 1950s. Thousands of them lined the plantations in neat rows, dripping their precious sap into buckets. Many of them were destroyed by napalm as the American military struggled to gain purchase. Amid the plantations and into the jungles beyond, the Vietcong had burrowed into tunnels that completely masked their presence. Operation Junction City was designed to uncover them, and to strike at the very heart of the enemy headquarters. It was anticipated that many thousands of Vietcong would be killed in the course of the operation.

Jim's company was engaged in jungle clearing, living in tent camps in the field, making their way through napalm-scorched land that sometimes burned the soles of their shoes. Snipers were ever present, appearing like mirages before fading back into the jungle.

Operation Junction City, launched with high expectations, ultimately failed because the Vietcong refused to engage. Rather than standing their ground and fighting it out with the Americans, they disappeared into Cambodia to regroup. Elusive and ever patient, the Vietcong challenged the fundamental strategies of war that involved huge displays of force. By the time the jungles were clear and the tunnels had been blasted open, the enemy was gone.

Home on leave after a year in Vietnam, Jim had never looked so good. He was striking in his uniform, the angles of his face sharpened and matured. His formerly slender arms were muscled and tanned. He was only nineteen, but he was unmistakably a man.

Eighteen months after we'd bid him good-bye, Jim had grown in stature, but his personality was more withdrawn. He didn't want to talk much about his experiences, and we didn't want to know. He had eighteen months to go on his three-year enlistment, but he announced that he was planning to make the army his career. After his leave, he'd be heading to Fort Carson, Colorado, to hone his skills as a combat demolition specialist.

One thing Jim *did* do on that visit was agree to give a talk to my high-school class and show some slides of Vietnam. I attended a Catholic academy for girls, and the presence of my handsome brother in his pressed army uniform sent a palpable thrill through the room—a near-swooning adulation that made Jim smile with embarrassment and pleasure. I was proud of him that day, proud of his confidence as he took questions from my classmates. Our teacher, Sister Albertina, stocky and aging, stood by his side, beaming with uncharacteristic delight.

"Were you afraid?" one girl asked in a trembling voice.

"Hell, yes," Jim said with a wide grin. He glanced, abashed, at Sister Albertina, apologizing for the curse. "Sorry, sister."

She smiled benevolently. "That's quite all right, dear." For once Jim could do no wrong.

After his presentation, my classmates swarmed around Jim, as if they were bees and he a honey pot, flirting and giggling and asking silly questions. I stood back, faintly amused and baffled. I had never seen my brother command such reverence.

It was a heady experience for Jim, this wave of approval. His uniform became a cloak of integrity, the visible evidence that he was part of something important. This was what he had always wanted, and now it was a reality.

Jim *was* brave, you had to give him that. For most soldiers in Vietnam, the calendar was their talisman. Counting down the days to the blessed rescue of 365, when they could board a plane for home and never look back. Not Jim. He always wanted more. After ten months in Colorado, he told our parents that he had volunteered for a second tour in Vietnam. They expressed pride, but privately they were fearful. By late 1968, the war was like a whirling dervish, the mission spinning out of control, the casualties mounting, and the nation rapidly turning sour.

The draft had reached a critical mass. I was old enough by then to know boys who carried draft cards and devised strategies to get out of serving. Today we may look back at draft dodging as a coward's choice, but at the time it was considered acceptable to avoid the draft if you could. The most patriotic, upstanding families in the nation were advising their sons to follow a path of deferments. During the Vietnam War, most people avoided the draft not by running but by rising—excelling at school or using family influence. When the draft lottery was instituted in 1969, those who received a high number breathed a sigh of relief and went on with their lives. In our own family, my brothers Greg and Paul both avoided Vietnam by enlisting in the navy and, by skill and intellect, earning assignments in peaceful areas of the world. Military service was a transient reality for them.

By the time Jim shipped out for his second tour, I was beginning my own transformation into a war protester. While Jim was humming "The Ballad of the Green Beret," I favored songs like the Beatles' "Give Peace a Chance" and Pete Seeger's "Where Have All the Flowers Gone?" I chanted with the crowds: "Hey, hey, LBJ, how many kids did you kill today?"

I shared my worries with Jim, attempting (foolishly, I now see) to have serious conversations with him about the legitimacy of the war. He simply could not comprehend my point of view. "That's your *brother* over there," he reminded me. "They want to *kill* us."

"Yes, but . . . well, isn't it *their* country?"

He stared at me as if I were an alien being.

I learned during those conversations that you couldn't be a good soldier and have doubts, because your doubts might get you killed. You couldn't be a good soldier and have a questioning mind. You took your orders and did your job.

It was a comfortable framework for my brother. Finally, after years of struggling to grasp the complex, contradictory rules of life, everything had been broken down to the most basic rule, and it was one he followed gladly. He was a soldier now. He could lay down the burden of his troubled childhood and march forward. And although he was collecting new burdens, they remained invisible. For now, he set one foot after the other along the trail of simple patriotism.

We were frozen in opposition—he a soldier, I a war protester. In later years, long after I had matured, married, and become a parent, Jim still spoke to me as if I were the wild-haired teenaged girl who chanted angry slogans at rallies. His resentment survived the decades. I was his Jane Fonda, the one who could never be forgiven.

Shortly after Jim arrived in Vietnam for a second year, assigned to the 87th Engineer Battalion, he was wounded in action. In an attack during a jungle clearing operation, his face was peppered with shrapnel. We were upset when we heard the news, although Jim assured us it was nothing. A couple of weeks in a hospital, and he went straight back to the field, his injuries not serious enough to earn him a ticket home. Others were not so lucky.

I've always regretted that we didn't know more about this injury and how it occurred. We have the Purple Heart, we have the letter from the army. But like all army awards, it's long on honor and short on details. All I can say is that by 1968 and 1969, Jim's war was taking on new dimensions. The military was at peak troop strength, with more than a half million Americans in-country, and the urgency of the war was ratcheted up by the building tensions at home. More than thirty thousand American troops had been killed in action to date, with the 1968 Tet Offensive taking the most deadly toll of the war. And still, there was little sense that progress was being made. The enemy refused to be conquered.

A photo of my brother in 1971 shows him standing in front of a stack of sand bags and chemical drums, unsmiling, rugged, and, somewhat surprisingly, wearing love beads. Welcome to the final days of the Vietnam War! By 1971, when Jim served his third and final tour with the 815th Engineer Battalion, there were only about 250,000 troops remaining in-country, shrinking by another 100,000 at the end of the year. Withdrawal was in the air, and so was Agent Orange. Jim was located at Camp Dillard, a rock quarry near Dalat, where his job was in soil analysis—essentially testing the results of the deadly chemical drops that rained from the sky. Close to the earth, the poison seeping into their skin and working its way into their bloodstreams, the army engineers suffered a silent toll that would kill many of them years after returning home. By one estimate, 70 percent of the engineers in Jim's battalion suffered repercussions from the effects of Agent Orange.

Troop morale was low. According to the army's own reports, about sixty thousand soldiers experimented with drugs during this period, seeking relief from the unsparing environment and the growing sense of futility. There were also over two hundred incidents of "fragging," in which unpopular officers were attacked with fragmentation grenades by men under their command. Base camps began to take on the aura of dissent—with peace signs carved into the burned earth, and long hair and love beads re-placing strict military dress code. Vietnam radio blasted Alice Cooper's "I gotta get out of this place." Another favorite was the Woodstock hit by Country Joe and the Fish, which had become a favorite with both the protesters and the soldiers:

Vietnam radio blasted Alice Cooper's "I gotta get out of this place," and Phil Ochs's "I Ain't Marching Anymore." Another fa-vorite was the Woodstock hit by Country Joe and the Fish, "I Feel like I'm Fixin' to Die Rag." The song involved a military-style sound-off, which the crowds loudly roared, but the message was decidedly anti-military: going to Vietnam was a short ticket to the grave. The lyrics evoked the growing sense of futility about the war's mission, and it became as popular with soldiers as it had been with protesters.

The antiwar movement had gained momentum, giving rise to radical groups such as the Weather Underground and Students for a Democratic Society (SDS). In Seattle, I joined five thousand other students at the University of Washington in protesting the war by marching down the middle of the I-5 freeway, stalling traffic at rush hour. Later, I found out that Dad was one of the commuters fuming in his car. He glared at me, the all-knowing parent: "You were there," he said, a fact not a question.

It may have been easy to discount the war protesters when they seemed composed entirely of lily-livered college kids. It was another matter entirely when the antiwar movement began to spread like a fast-moving brush fire through the military bases and among the veteran population. The early seventies saw dramatic challenges to military discipline on virtually every base. From Camp Pendleton, California, to Fort Benning, Georgia, to Fort Sam Houston, Texas, to Fort Dix, New Jersey, soldiers were breaking ranks to attend rallies headlined by Abbie Hoffman, Jane Fonda, and Tom Hayden. They were participating in marches organized by Vietnam Veterans Against the War. Many engaged in acts of civil disobedience that landed them inthe brink.

It was during this period that a young veteran named John Kerry testified before the Senate Foreign Relations Committee, and spoke the words that would remain a subject of controversy for more than thirty years: "How do you ask a man to be the last man to die in Vietnam? How do you ask a man to die for a mistake?"

Twelve thousand miles away in Vietnam, disillusionment with the mission mingled with a deeply felt resentment toward the unsupportive population back home, a resentment that is still felt by many veterans today, who blame the antiwar movement for killing the spirit of the war and leaving them stranded in the jungle. It's fair to say that soldiers rely not just on the cohesion of their brethren on the battlefield, but also on a cohesion back home—the sure knowledge that their nation supports them.

By the time the last troops returned in 1975, the exhausted nation longed for a true end, the kind of finality found in forgetting. We jammed the complex emotions into the far recesses of our minds, not wanting to relive the awful moment when those helicopters with their desperate cargo lifted off Asian soil. Fleeing, cutting and running, and losing a war for the first time in our memory.

The silence was deafening. That was the worst part of the aftermath of the war. The nation had moved on, barely sparing a second glance at the soldiers who had fought. The sons and daughters of the Greatest Generation slunk back to civilian life, expected to go on as if nothing had happened, or, like their fathers, just pick up the old can-do spirit and live the American dream. But for many of them, the dream was a nightmare.

It wasn't getting spit upon; by all accounts those experiences were few and far between. It was the silence, the not wanting to know. It was the pity and mild contempt. It was the concerted effort by family and friends to change the subject. It was the complete absence of a pat on the back for a job well done, or even the sentiment that it had been a job worth doing. It was the way soldiers were greeted not as heroes but as strangers— and worse, as if they'd done something wrong in going to war on our behalf.

As the saying goes, "Success has a thousand fathers; failure is an orphan."

A 1979 national opinion poll found that only 20 percent of the public thought our military engagement in Vietnam was the right thing to have done. Sixty-three percent thought Vietnam veterans were "suckers" for having risked their lives there.

There were, of course, no parades. We didn't know how to honor the soldiers of that failed war, so we simply closed the book.

After the Iran hostages were freed in 1981, many veterans resented the grand ticker-tape parade in New York City that was held in their honor. "People called them heroes," one vet told me, "but they were just victims. What were we—shit?"

Jim shared that view. "I'll bet you were at that big parade for the Iran hostages," he said to me when we were together that year for a family event. I was living in New York by then, and indeed, I had attended, wanting to experience an old-fashioned ticker-tape parade among the skyscrapers of lower Manhattan. It was pretty exhilarating. I told Jim I'd been there.

"Yeah," he said, smiling with satisfaction at having his opinion of me confirmed once again. "You wouldn't have showed up for *our* parade."

I started to protest, but he cut me off. "Because there *was* no parade," he shouted. "We got spat on instead."

"Jim, seriously, did anyone ever spit on you?" I asked.

He shook his head and stared down, not meeting my eyes. "You just have no idea. Why do I even bother?"

This was the trajectory of all our conversations. I could not fathom Jim's depths. He was as inscrutable as a plaster cast. But I didn't really want to understand. In my mind, the war was over. And that was my problem, not Jim's. The great myth of war is that it can be left behind.

FOUR

DUST IN
THE WIND

THE EMOTIONAL FALLOUT of war is seldom given its due. We prefer to cling to a more sentimental picture, the reality of battle and its aftermath quickly forgotten. We revel in the moment when Johnny, or Jim, or Jane comes marching home.

The enduring images at the end of World War II are cemented in the public's memory—the unabated joy, the cheering crowds, the kiss between a sailor and a nurse in Times Square forever captured in an iconic Eisenstaedt photograph. For millions, that photo symbolizes the thrill of victory, another Great War won, sailors returned home from sea.

Everyone was glad to be done with the carnage, to have survived to live another day. Americans were eager to get back home to raise their families and wash away the bad memories with a healthy dose of good old American productivity. The months and years at war were like dust in the wind, quickly dissipating and drifting away.

This is the central narrative of the Greatest Generation—a vast population of citizen soldiers who shucked off their uniforms, put down their guns, and returned to their roles as civilians with barely a look back at the dark catacombs of a bloody war. They lived remarkably industrious lives. By the labor of their hands, America became the preeminent superpower. These

veterans didn't dwell on the horrors of war, and they were ad-
mired for their stoicism. Their ability to seamlessly shift gears
from the foxholes to the suburban tract homes that sprung up in
the 1950s was a testament to their discipline and dignity.

By contrast, their children, the baby boomers, were charac-
terized as weak and pampered, the "Me Generation." The veterans of Vietnam were cast as a shaggy crew of miscreants, an
anomaly in America's military history. Many of them opposed the
war, even while they were on active duty, and when they returned
home, they vigorously pursued claims against the government—
post-traumatic stress disorder, illnesses caused by exposure to
Agent Orange—and they wouldn't shut up about it. They weren't
welcome at VFW halls, with their long hair and shabby fatigue
jackets, but that didn't matter because they didn't want to be
there anyway.

Two generations. Two disparate stories. There's only one problem. The story that has been told about the Greatest Generation
isn't entirely true.

Evidence has surfaced that World War II veterans paid a
tremendous emotional price—perhaps even greater than that of
both World War I and Vietnam veterans—and the cover-up was
carefully managed to give the impression that they were psychologically unaffected by the traumas of war.

During the post–World War II years, there was a construction boom in veterans hospitals—vast, impersonal structures
housing thousands upon thousands of physically and emotionally wounded veterans. By one account, fully 60 percent of postwar VA patients were psychiatric. Unfortunately, there were few
treatments available at that time for the invisible wounds of war.
Many patients spent years in hospital wards, reliving their individual horrors over and over again, unable to escape the aftermath of their experiences. Cigarettes were often the primary

medication prescribed to deal with the shakes. "Take six packs of Camels a day, and don't call me in the morning."

Those years were the heyday of lobotomies, a promising new treatment that tended to bring around the most severely traumatized veterans, or, at least, make them more placid and manageable. The famous "ice pick" method, invented by Dr. Walter J. Freeman, chief of neurology at George Washington University Hospital, quickly and efficiently disrupted the functioning of the front temporal lobe, where memories and emotions were centered. The most violent, disruptive patients quieted down immediately after surgery. Lobotomy was thought to be a miracle, a real advance in the treatment of traumatized veterans and other severely disturbed people. (President Kennedy's sister Rosemary was subjected to a lobotomy during that period, leaving her calm but nonfunctional for the rest of her life.) The VA embraced lobotomies as a means of restoring combat fatigued soldiers to full capacity, so they could lead normal lives.

The failures of this brutal surgical solution are now well documented, but between 1943 and 1951, the VA approved lobotomies for more than three thousand psychologically disturbed soldiers. Experts now speculate that it was a dread of this procedure that kept so many World War II veterans silent about their mental and emotional problems.

And so it is that the horrific secrets of our fathers' war are only now beginning to come to light. Here is one particularly shocking story.

My friend Jeff called me one day, eager to tell me about his father. Jeff's voice on the phone was excited and disturbed. Thirty years after his father died of cancer, Jeff decided to order a copy of his military records. He knew little of his father's service, except that he'd joined the army in 1941 as a seventeen-year-old, right out of high school, and had briefly served in Italy before being declared missing in action. For almost a year, his status as "missing" was maintained, until magically, one day he was "found" and returned to his home. Soon after, he'd met and married Jeff's mother, and settled down to raise a family—Jeff and his three siblings—in suburban Philadelphia. He rarely spoke of his service after that time. Jeff knew only the bare account, although his grandmother occasionally referred to the frantic year when army representatives would regularly show up on her doorstep to report that there was still no news, how she grew to accept that her boy was probably dead, and finally, her overwhelming joy and amazement at his return. By the time she received the news that her son was alive, she was so delirious with relief that she didn't care about the details. It was enough to have him back.

Growing up, Jeff never thought the story was strange, and he didn't dare press for details. His father was a strong, silent man, a good father and provider, whose occasional flashes of anger and long brooding silences were evidence of deeper agonies that no one, least of all his children, wanted to unleash. When he died at age forty, the family mourned him and eventually moved on.

In recent years, Jeff, the parent of two children, had grown curious about his father's wartime experience. He wondered if the military records would reveal more about the period in which he was missing in action and how he was found. Jeff imagined a dramatic story of rescue and return, his own family's version of *Saving Private Ryan*. In his wildest dreams, he couldn't have imagined the tale told by his father's military records.

The shocking revelation contained in the pages was this: Jeff's father had never been missing at all. Barely a month into his service, in the aftermath of a battle that killed a beloved officer who had been his mentor and protector, Jeff's father had a complete nervous breakdown. He was shipped home to Pennsylvania, where he spent nearly a year in a mental hospital, only twenty miles from his mother's house. Rather than telling his mother the truth, so she could sit at his bedside, the army maintained the fiction that he was lost—and in a sense he was.

Jeff could not fathom the enormity of the secret, or the justification for the subterfuge. He pored over the records, seeking clarity. But there was no one left to ask, and the records were silent on who ordered the cover-up.

"Who were they trying to spare by perpetrating this lie?" Jeff wondered. "Don't tell me it was my grandmother. She would have happily welcomed back her son, no matter how broken he was. She had a right to be at his side. The only possible explanation I can think of is that they wanted to hide the extent of the mental trauma being suffered by soldiers. I'm sure my dad wasn't an isolated case."

War is hell. That is an external fact. It is also an internal reality. Emotional trauma might be an expected outcome, yet it has rarely been treated as such. Worse, there has traditionally been a strong bias toward characterizing psychic wounds as a coward's resort, a moral weakness that cannot be tolerated in the midst of battle.

After World War I, unable to comprehend why so many soldiers suffered from "shell shock" or "battle fatigue," the military concluded that these soldiers had preexisting conditions that made them unable to cope with the stresses of war. Determined to minimize or even eliminate the problem, the military began an aggressive program to screen out potential mental cases before they enlisted. In effect, the military was proposing that mental trauma was an *abnormality* in the course of war, rather than the reaction of a *normal* person faced with the abnormal circumstances of war. Those who fought in World War II were presumed to be mentally fit, one and all—a condition that was expected to hold throughout the war.

General George Patton certainly believed that. Patton's love of the battlefield is well known. Patton, with his double-holstered, pearl-handled pistols and martinet's strut, was lionized as a great soldier, a true leader of men in battle. Patton helped perpetuate a mythic ideal of courage in combat. In two incidents that are rarely mentioned anymore, Patton attacked traumatized soldiers so cruelly that he later received a reprimand, and nearly lost his command.

According to eyewitness reports, Patton entered a tent filled with wounded soldiers waiting to be evacuated, and began to speak to them. As he went from man to man offering his appreciation for their service, he approached one young man huddled in a corner, shivering. The youngster showed no apparent external wounds. Patton approached and asked what was wrong with him. The boy, hardly able to compose himself, finally spit out, "It's my nerves," and began to sob, his entire body shaking.

Patton was enraged. He screamed at the cowering man, "Your nerves? Hell, you are just a goddamned coward, you yellow son of a bitch!" He then slapped the man and said, "Shut up that goddamned crying! I won't have these brave men here who have been shot at seeing a yellow bastard sitting here crying." He struck the man a second time.

Patton then ordered the medical officer, "Don't admit this yellow bastard. There's nothing the matter with him. I won't have the hospitals cluttered up with these sons of bitches who haven't got the guts to fight."

He said to the cowering man, "You're going back to the front lines, and you may get shot and killed, but you're going to fight. If you don't, I'll stand you up against a wall and have a firing squad kill you on purpose. In fact," he added, reaching for his pistol, "I ought to shoot you myself, you goddamned whimpering coward."

On another occasion, Patton was visiting wounded soldiers in a hospital in Sicily when he came upon a young soldier sitting on the edge of his cot, crying.

Patton asked, "What's wrong, soldier, are you hurt?"

The soldier buried his face in his hands and sobbed that he was not hurt, but he couldn't take it anymore.

Patton ordered him to stand up. The soldier got to his feet and the general slapped him across the neck with his gloves, which he was carrying, and said, "Why don't you act like a man instead of a damn sniveling baby? Look at these severely wounded soldiers, not complaining a bit and as cheerful as can be, and here you are, a goddamned crybaby."

Although these incidents were witnessed by many people, they were not initially reported in the press. A group of correspondents was persuaded not to publish the stories when they were told that the publicity would hurt the war effort, diminish Patton's authority, and harm morale. Months after the fact, correspondent Drew Pearson made the story public, but his account never gained much traction. Patton went on to be honored as a clear example of the right kind of leadership in a war zone. His stance reinforced the idea that the ability to harden one's heart and soul to killing was the definition of courage. Expressing emotional distress at the sight of carnage was the definition of cowardice. That's why we hear so little about psychological trauma among World War II veterans.

However, the truth has begun to emerge as the ticking time bomb of post-traumatic stress disorder has quietly exploded in elderly veterans. Deeply buried in the brains, hearts, and psyches of these men is a secret shame they've tried to ignore but no longer can. Delayed PTSD is frequently cited by doctors, nurses, and therapists treating geriatric patients.

According to Paula Schnurr, PhD, who works with the VA's National Center for Post-Traumatic Stress Disorder in Vermont,

"Every clinician I know who has worked with older vets has talked about having a number of these cases—people who have never had problems with PTSD and then suddenly, in old age, have to come in for treatment. But the data on this phenomenon are lacking."

Few studies have attempted to tackle this population. One that has is an Australian study of World War II veterans almost sixty years after the war, conducted by researcher Margaret Lindorff, which demonstrates how a strong cultural resistance to seeking help masked the psychic wounds of battle, but did not eliminate them. Lindorff surveyed 116 men, ages seventy-five to ninety-one, many of whom had fought in the Isurava Battle on the Kokoda Track in Papua New Guinea in 1942.

It was a particularly devastating encounter. Seven hundred men fought a four-day battle against approximately ten thousand Japanese soldiers, suffering enormous casualties before being forced to withdraw.

Sixty years later, Lindorff's survey respondents detailed life-long problems with concentration, sleep disturbances, nightmares, flashbacks, intrusive thoughts, and emotional distress. Lindorff reported that the most consistent theme was avoidance. Only two of the men had ever sought help for any of their symptoms.

To understand how it is possible for an individual to suffer the onset of psychological trauma many decades after the fact, one must grasp the insidious nature of post-traumatic stress. It can manifest itself immediately, or it can hide, like a slow-growing virus, only to emerge in response to a triggering event. For aging World War II and Korean War veterans, the process follows a familiar pattern: A man comes back from war, settles down with a job and family, and immerses himself in the gratifying process of living, loving, and producing. He draws his meaning from his many contributions—raising children, working hard, making friends, worshipping at his local church or temple.

But as he ages, the supportive center of the life he has crafted begins to fall away. His children leave home, he retires, perhaps suffers a heart attack; his wife dies and leaves him entirely alone. The network crumbles. It is at this point that the virus of war springs to malevolent life. He begins to have nightmares. His hands shake when he drives a car. He grows depressed. He begins to drink.

Sadly, while PTSD in an aging veteran population may be common, it is rarely acknowledged. When an elderly man exhibits signs of stress, it is too easy to blame natural deterioration. There's an entire generation that never sought counseling or took antidepressants or antianxiety medications, and they aren't about to start now.

So they suffer in silence. I think about my father. I have no way of knowing whether or not he experienced PTSD later in life. What I do know is that after he retired and his children left home, my father changed from a cheerful, confident, happy man to a quiet, sometimes depressed, man. When he became ill, his depression worsened. It was hard to watch my joking, energetic dad fall silent, and I might never have thought of PTSD had it not been for a story my mother told me, just recently.

The day before he died, Dad was sitting in the backyard, my mother beside him. It was a warm August afternoon. Dad was weak, but he felt good that day. There was no sign that it would be his last. Suddenly, he turned to my mother, his face heavy with sadness. "I really miss my buddies," he said.

It was a small moment, but it stayed with Mom. She knew he was talking about the men on the ship, long ago, who smiled out from the pictures Dad kept in an old album. Young men, in navy whites, together in struggle and victory—the memory of those days forever a dull ache in my father's heart.

"To kill another human being, to take another life out of this world with one pull of a trigger, is something that never leaves you. It is as if a part of you dies with them. If you choose to keep on living, there may be healing, and even hope and happiness again—but that scar and memory and sorrow will be with you forever."

The author of these words is sixty-year-old Ron Kovic, the paralyzed Vietnam veteran whose searing account of the war, *Born on the Fourth of July*, gained him wide acclaim. Oliver Stone's movie based on the book, starring Tom Cruise as Kovic, won an Academy Award. Kovic, who was paralyzed from the chest down in combat, wrote his story thirty-five years ago on a manual type-writer in Santa Monica, California. Today he is an activist on be-half of veterans, sounding a warning that while the visible scars of war can cripple, the emotional scars are just as long-lasting and just as debilitating.

Post-traumatic stress syndrome was not accepted as an offi-cial diagnostic category by the VA until five years after the end of the Vietnam War. In the twenty-eight years since it was entered into the manual of psychiatric disorders, it remains poorly un-derstood, in part because its symptoms are so varied and can be unpredictable.

The symptoms of PTSD fall into three general categories. The first category involves symptoms related to reliving the traumatic event. These include flashbacks, nightmares, and extreme emo-tional and physical reactions to reminders of the event. Emotional reactions can include feeling guilty, extreme fear of harm, or the numbing of emotions. Physical reactions can include uncontrol-lable shaking, inability to catch one's breath, the chills, heart pal-pitations, and headaches so intense they cause nausea.

The second way PTSD is expressed is through detachment—avoiding activities, places, thoughts, or feelings that might recall or be related to the trauma; becoming increasingly estranged from others; depression; and the effort to numb thoughts and memories through alcohol and/or drugs.

The third most common expression of PTSD is a state of arousal—hypervigilance, difficulty sleeping, irritability, outbursts of anger, panic attacks, or an inability to concentrate and focus.

At least ten thousand new PTSD claims have been filed by Vietnam veterans since the start of operations in Afghanistan and Iraq. These veterans claim that the constant deluge of stories and pictures from the combat zones have caused extreme emotional and psychic distress. In 2006, former senator Max Cleland, a well-known Vietnam veteran and triple amputee, courageously went public about his decision to seek treatment for PTSD. Cleland cited the Iraq War as the trigger. "I realize my symptoms are avoidance, not wanting to connect with anything dealing with the war, tremendous sadness over the casualties that are taken, a real identification with that . . . I've tried to disconnect and disassociate from the media. I don't watch it as much. I'm not engrossed in it like I was," he said. Cleland added that the same thing is happening to Vietnam veterans all over America.

The physiological dynamics that make PTSD possible are embedded in our ancient stress mechanisms, which are necessary for survival. We can easily imagine an ancestor, say one hundred thousand years ago, encountering terrible danger. A threatening animal leaps in his path, and instantaneously he experiences a burst of adrenaline. His heart starts pumping, sending blood to his muscles. This is the fight-or-flight response, which shifts all of his energy toward survival. There is no question that this finely tuned physiological response has been essential throughout human history, and it is absolutely crucial in times of war. However, because it is impossible to remain in a high-adrenaline state, our central nervous system has two complementary parts. The sympathetic nervous system charges into action when there is danger; the parasympathetic nervous system restores calm when the danger has passed. Chronic stress occurs when there is no opportunity for recovery from the high adrenaline state. It becomes constant, even after the specific incident of danger is over. This isn't just a "mental" state, where one imagines danger where it does not exist. It's a complete physiological state over which the individual has little immediate control. It can manifest itself in many ways. For example, John Horton, MD, a California doctor who specializes in chronic stress disorders, told me of an Iraq War veteran he treated. Mark Z. was a captain in the army who came to Dr. Horton because he was suffering from severe intestinal problems. He told Dr. Horton that he had been very upset by the uncertain mission and chaotic setting he found in Iraq. He was also tremendously affected by the number of civilian casualties, and felt a great deal of guilt. It literally tore at his gut. Halfway through his tour, he became quite ill and ended up back in the States.

"Mark's intestinal problems were real," Dr. Horton said. "He didn't make them up. But clearly the basis was extreme stress. My colleague Eda Hanzelik and I often treat veterans at our clinic whose post-traumatic stress is manifested in digestive disorders, heart problems, thyroid disease, chronic headaches, and many other physical disabilities. When the stress syndrome is treated, the physical problems sometimes disappear completely."

Ignorance about the nature of PTSD can show up in some pretty surprising quarters. For example, one person who should know better is Cindy McCain, wife of Senator John McCain, a former prisoner of war in Vietnam. During McCain's 2008 presidential run, Cindy gave this interview to *Marie Claire* magazine:

Q: You met your husband after his POW days. To what
   extent is that still with you—or is it a part of
   history?

McCAIN: My husband will be the first one to tell you
   that that's in the past. Certainly it's a part of who he
   is, but he doesn't dwell on it. It's not part of a daily
   experience that we experience or anything like that.
   But it has shaped him. It has made him the leader
   that he is.

Q: But no cold sweats in the middle of the night?

McCAIN: Oh, no, no, no, no, no. My husband, he'd be
   the first one to tell you that he was trained to do
   what he was doing. The guys who had the trouble
   were the 18-year-olds who were drafted. He was
   trained, he went to the Naval Academy, he was a
   trained United States naval officer, and so he knew
   what he was doing.

In other words, only teenage draftees were subject to PTSD.
Training, maturity, and perhaps character, would shield against it.
Cindy McCain, who undoubtedly was trying to offer reassurances
that her husband was mentally sound, managed to insult the dignity of countless veterans who struggle with debilitating emotional trauma, regardless of how well trained they were or how
heroically they performed in battle.

Furthermore, despite the substantial body of scientific evidence that supports the insidious effects of PTSD on people who
have served in combat, there are still those outliers intent on
characterizing traumatized veterans as slackers. Leading the current charge is a woman named Sally Satel, a scholar with the
American Enterprise Institute, a conservative think tank, and co-
author of *One Nation Under Therapy*. Satel takes issue with the

very idea that soldiers are traumatized by war. Rather, she argues that most of those who claim to suffer from PTSD actually have behavioral and substance-abuse problems completely "unrelated to battle." Satel also repeats a theory about psychological trauma that has been consistently discredited by experts. That is, you either see it at the time it occurs, or you don't. It's either there on the battlefield, or it doesn't exist.

Satel, who testified before Congress about the "myth" of PTSD, cautioned lawmakers that many if not most PTSD claims were motivated by the desire for payment. "There is an economic incentive to claim suffering," she said. "A veteran deemed to be fully disabled by post-traumatic stress disorder can collect two thousand to three thousand dollars a month tax-free."

If Satel were to be proven correct—and the VA's own studies strongly dispute her position—one would have to believe that the claimants are masochists. No one who has ever filed a claim for PTSD would characterize it as the easy way out. Indeed, the process is so convoluted and intimidating that it is, by itself, a new form of trauma. The VA places the veteran claiming this disorder in the position of having to relive the incident, analyze its impact, and recall names, dates, and places that may be months or years in the past. The first step in the claims process involves filling out a twenty-six page form, including a detailed essay on the exact moment or event that caused PTSD.

But PTSD is not like a shrapnel wound that pierces your skin at a precise moment in time. It may develop over the course of repeated combat experiences. As one soldier, returned from Iraq, put it, "I think the whole year over there was my stressor."

The task of filling out a claim for PTSD is especially difficult for veterans of prior wars, when twenty, thirty, or more years have passed before something went *click*, and everything blew up in their faces. Furthermore, one of the primary symptoms of PTSD is a concerted effort to block the traumatic event from memory.

There are so many roadblocks on the way to a successful PTSD claim that some vets just give up. Some die before their claims have made it through the lengthy process. Some spend years in the wasteland of appeals for claims that were denied. Satel's supposed disability gravy train is nowhere in sight.

Although the VA pays lip service to its interest in helping veterans who suffer from PTSD, in a military culture where stoicism is so highly prized, PTSD is an ongoing blight, hugely expensive and complicated. And just as the VA was struggling through a backlog of cases from the Vietnam and Gulf wars, current wars began to unleash an overwhelming load on the system.

A 2006 e-mail from Norma J. Perez, the PTSD coordinator at a VA facility in Temple, Texas, exposed the VA's difficulty in handling the load. Ms. Perez wrote to her subordinates, "Given that we have more and more compensation seeking veterans, I'd like to suggest that you refrain from giving a diagnosis of PTSD straight out. Consider a diagnosis of adjustment disorder, RO [ruling out] PTSD . . . we really don't have time to do the extensive testing that should be done to determine PTSD."

In other words, when the cost of treating PTSD becomes too great, just call it something else. Here's one example:

Since 2003, the military has discharged more than 22,000 combat soldiers for "personality disorders," making them ineligible for medical care and disability payments. Typically, these soldiers experienced some form of trauma related to their service, the most common being a nearly invisible but devastating form of brain injury that results from being in close proximity to an exploding bomb. By classifying these injuries as personality disorders, the military has saved an estimated $8 billion in disability benefits and $5 billion in medical care.

It's a betrayal. There's no other word for it. .

Imagine this scenario: You enlist in the army and are sent to Iraq. You serve honorably and with great courage. One day your battalion headquarters is blasted by rocket fire with an explosive force that hurls you into a wall, shatters your eardrums, and sends your brain slamming around your skull like an out-of-control pinball machine. Tiny bits of shrapnel pierce your head and neck, leaving superficial wounds. But it is the interior trauma that plays havoc with your brain. You can't think straight, your mind is in a fog, and you're depressed. You can't concentrate.

You return to the States, where you undergo extensive medical testing. The tests conclude that you are no longer battle ready. But instead of the obvious diagnosis—traumatic brain injury, suffered in combat—you are discharged as a "5-13," separation due to personality disorder. In effect, the military doctors have determined that the rocket fire was not the cause of your disability, but merely the trigger for preexisting emotional problems. And how do they make that determination? Do they interview family and friends? Do they examine old school records? Do they have information revealing a prior dysfunction? Do they perform due diligence? No. It would seem not. The diagnosis forever remains a mystery.

And what could be the motivation for such a large number of combat soldiers being discharged with "preexisting" personality disorders? The inescapable conclusion is that it's a financial calculation. Soldiers discharged as 5-13s are not eligible for health benefits or disability pay. To add insult to injury, if a soldier is discharged for a personality disorder before he has served his full time, he must return a portion of his signing bonus. Many of these soldiers leave the service in debt, owing the army thousands of dollars.

The Suicide Wall is not made of polished black granite. You cannot visit this memorial. It exists in hearts and minds and in cyberspace. The Suicide Wall, posted on the Internet, is an effort to record the names and stories of Vietnam veterans who have committed suicide since the war. Alexander Paul, who has written about soldier suicide, started the site in lieu of an actual white marble wall he proposed for construction in Washington, D.C.

Such a wall will never be built. But Alexander's electronic version is powerful and moving. Scrolling down the list of names, each one a veteran who took his own life, is yet another reminder of the sobering cost of war.

On the Suicide Wall, we read of Moses Addison, who died by a self-inflicted gunshot wound to the head in 2005, leaving behind a wife and five children. He was fifty-nine, and served in Vietnam forty years earlier.

Or Victor Boyett, whose second suicide attempt in 1997 by drug overdose was successful. He had endured chronic pain, seizures, headaches, and depression from a neck injury suffered while he served in the navy. Family members write that part of his depression was due to his failure to receive recognition of his total disability from the navy and the VA.

Then there is Gary Hawker, a marine in Vietnam, who died of a self-inflicted gunshot wound to the chest in 1999. An old comrade writes that Hawker was "another veteran who was lost for so many years, and could not find peace and worth. The VA was trying to help, but about thirty years too late. Hope that he may find his inner peace wherever all heroes go. And that all of his friends will try and understand. Semper Fi."

Larry Loundree died in 1999 of asphyxiation from an exhaust pipe. His sad decline is recounted by his brother: "My brother Larry was a loner and very confrontational. He cut himself off from his whole family, living a lonely and miserable life the last few years. He served in the Navy as a radar specialist on the U.S.S. Chicago. Was stationed in the Bay of Tonkin. He came home different. He then went to work at Reynolds Metals where he stayed 25 yrs. When they closed down he took his retirement early at 45 yrs. He lived on Mt. Hood and just became very reclusive. He maintained one close relationship but not family. The one friend informed him she was moving the next summer to marry her boyfriend and went on vacation leaving Larry to watch her home. When she came back in 5 days he was nowhere around and after a few days we knew something was wrong. He drove himself up on one of the many spur roads and just went to sleep. He never discussed being in the Navy and we never really thought Vietnam would have affected him like someone on the front line."

One after another, these brief, touching tributes by families, friends, and comrades have a strangely cathartic effect for those left behind. One likes to think that their fallen brothers would have found comfort in knowing that someone cared.

The reality of service-related suicide, whether it's on the battlefield or at home, brings us to a terrible point of reckoning. We may not be able to understand what is inside the heart of a person who takes his or her own life. But we can't ignore it.

Greg Mitchell, author of *So Wrong for So Long*, an indictment of the press coverage of the lead-up to the Iraq War, and the editor of *Editor and Publisher* magazine, has been one of the rare voices sounding an alarm about suicide among those serving in Iraq and Afghanistan. "Why isn't the press on a suicide watch?" he asks, citing a startling spike in incidents since the start of the Iraq War. The army's own statistics show that every day of the war, five U.S. soldiers try to kill themselves. At least 3 percent of deaths in Iraq are due to self-inflicted gunshot wounds.

Greg is a longtime friend and neighbor of mine, normally a soft-spoken man, a husband and father who is a familiar figure on the Little League baseball fields of our river town community. But when Greg talks about soldier suicides, his temper flares. On a June evening in 2008, when a few of us gathered at the local library to talk about the cost of the Iraq War, Greg's mind was on the latest soldier suicide, that of Private Eugene Kanakaole.

The young soldier's death struck a particular chord with me, as he was serving with my brother's old battalion—the 87th Engineers—in Iraq when he died of a self-inflicted gunshot wound to the head. "He was only nineteen," Greg said, his voice a mix of indignation and despair. "A teenager. And did his suicide make news? Not a word."

Suicide in a combat posting is rarely classified as such, at least initially. The official classification of the death may be "non-combat-related," and the details might be long in coming—maybe never, especially if the family doesn't really want to know them. In monitoring incidents of suicide by military personnel, the press faces an uphill battle due to the wall of silence erected by both the military and the families. There is a shame associated with suicide, and the families of those who've committed suicide are understandably resistant to media coverage.

Suicide at war is horrible to contemplate. Suicide in the aftermath of war is just plain sad. Earlier in the year, Greg had written about a local man named Steve Vickerman, who served two tours in Iraq with the Marine Corps Reserve, and returned home with deeper emotional wounds than he could endure. He suffered a mental breakdown, and hanged himself. Greg sometimes feels like a voice crying in the wilderness. When will the media pick up the charge? And when will the VA tell the truth about the rising number of suicides?

A lawsuit filed by veteran organizations against the Department of Veterans Affairs unveiled a deliberate and drastic underreporting of the number of suicides in the population of active and retired military under the VA's care.

The cover-up was first reported by CBS News, when its independent investigation seemed at odds with the official VA counts. Dr. Ira Katz, head of mental health for the VA, told CBS that there had been about 790 suicide attempts in 2007. But CBS's estimate was much higher, more like six thousand. The truth was even worse, and it might never have come to light had an e-mail written by Katz not been leaked to the news division at CBS.

The e-mail, addressed to Katz's top medical adviser, read: "Shhh! Our suicide prevention coordinators are identifying about 1,000 suicide attempts per month among veterans we see in our medical facilities . . . This is something we should (carefully) address ourselves in some sort of release before someone stumbles on it."

Alarmed by the report, in May 2008, the House Veterans Committee held a hearing called "The Truth About Veteran Suicides." The hearing revealed a callous disregard for the potential for suicide among active military and veterans. One high official with the VA's health-care operations was quoted as saying, "Suicide rates are not a metric we're measuring . . . Suicide occurs like cancer occurs."

Testifying before Congress, Penny Coleman, the widow of a Vietnam veteran who committed suicide, and the author of *Flashback: Posttraumatic Stress Disorder, Suicide, and the Lessons of War,* told lawmakers: "Since the start of the Iraq War, the backlog of unanswered disability claims has grown from 325,000 to more than 600,000, with 800,000 new claims expected in each of the next two years. On average, a veteran must wait almost six months to have a claim heard. If a veteran loses and appeals a case, it usually takes almost two years to resolve. It is worth noting that if a service member or a veteran dies while an appeal is pending, the appeal dies as well."

The warning signs are loud and clear for a new generation of soldiers. Each war carries its own special traumas, but the men and women serving in Iraq and Afghanistan have unique challenges that didn't exist in Vietnam. Chief among them is the Pentagon's decision to extend tours from twelve to fifteen months in order to support the surge. In addition, time between deployments has been shortened to twelve months, and many soldiers have served three or four tours of duty in the Middle East— including husbands and wives who served at the same time, and mothers of infants. This has created a stress on individuals and families that even the VA acknowledges is disturbing.

Worse still, in 2006, the Pentagon released new guidelines, allowing commanders to redeploy soldiers suffering from "a psychiatric disorder in remission, or whose residual symptoms do not impair duty performance." The presumption that PTSD is treatable, in the same way that, say, high blood pressure is treatable, and that "remission" is an appropriate term for a psychiatric patient who has stabilized with treatment, reveals a startling lack of understanding of PSTD. Given the stresses that accompany a return to battle, how likely is it that these individuals will not snap?

Twenty percent of married troops in Iraq say they are planning a divorce. Forty percent of returning soldiers say they feel like "a guest in their own home." Alienation, depression, and the sense that even their loved ones cannot understand them increase the pressures already building inside from their experiences at war. As of 2009, forty thousand Iraq and Afghanistan veterans have been treated for substance abuse at VA hospitals. It well may be the tip of a very deep iceberg.

The VA clearly does not have a system in place to address the crisis of suicide among military personnel. A 2008 report by the House Veterans Committee showed that 90.9 percent of VA facilities do not have suicide case managers. And the screening for suicide risk is perfunctory, consisting of two questions:

- Have you felt depressed or hopeless in the last two
  weeks?
- Have you thought about hurting or harming
  yourself in the last two weeks?

If the answer to the second question is no, there is no additional screening. So, according to the VA, as long as you haven't thought about killing yourself in the last couple of weeks, you're A-OK.

At the National Institute of Mental Health, director Thomas Insel offered a disturbing prediction—that suicide and psychiatric mortality could trump combat death in Afghanistan and Iraq. Insel based his opinion on a study published by the RAND Corporation think tank, which reported that approximately 300,000 new veterans suffer from PTSD, and another 320,000 have sustained a traumatic brain injury. The study found that only half of these soldiers sought treatment for their injuries.

According to official VA statistics, 20,000 Vietnam veterans have committed suicide—by any measure an unacceptable percentage of those who served. Off the record, however, a retired VA doctor estimates that the number is closer to 200,000. We'll never know for sure, but the doctor paints a picture we can all understand—of single car accidents late at night with no one to bear witness, of accidents with guns in the woods, of drug overdoses in lonely apartments. They leave behind the broken hearts of their loved ones, who do not know how to make sense of it.

This letter is from a young woman in Texas:

I am thirty-two, and I lost my father recently to a gun shot in the head—suicide. I am in pain and angry at the Vietnam War. I may not have fought the war, but I felt my father's anger, depression, isolation, and sickness with Agent Orange and other problems.

When I was a little girl, he would get so angry and his eyes would glaze over. He would get in a tackle position and run after us and beat us until he came back to reality. He was not there—he was in Vietnam all over again. I was called a "motherfucker" if I complained about anything: "You mother-fuckers don't know how good you have it."

I realized as a small child that my dad would just go nuts and it wasn't his fault. I would feel his pain and remorse; it would run through my body. Now he is gone. I accept the fact that he just didn't want to suffer anymore, but I'm still here and I still feel the pain. I know I am not alone in this.

——

FIVE

FULL RETREAT

1984

IT WAS A JUNE wedding. Our entire family had gathered, all nine of my parents' children together in one place for the first time in many years. Our brother John, then twenty, was getting married, and Jim made a rare appearance for the event.

Long gone were the days when our political differences about a war in Asia had steamed up the windows with the heat of our arguments. We'd grown past it, settled into our lives, and become more concerned with the practical matters of jobs and families.

I was living in New York by then, amicably divorced, working and raising my ten-year-old son, Paul. I didn't travel to Seattle much—maybe a couple of times a year so Paul could get to know his extended family. My parents were still busy raising young children of their own, the last of their brood. Eighteen-year-old Margy and sixteen-year-old Joanne still lived at home.

But the real guest of honor at John's wedding celebration was Jim, who seldom visited. He had been stationed in many places since the Vietnam War and was just ending a three-year stint with the Berlin Brigade in Germany. Berlin was a bustling, cosmopolitan city that had been rebuilt from the rubble of World War II. In the decade before the fall of the Berlin Wall, it was considered great duty, and Jim had often written glowingly of the experience. The country itself held special interest for Dad, who was of German heritage but had never been there. After the wedding, Jim would head to his new posting at Fort Hood in Killeen, Texas.

The minute Jim walked in the door, it was clear that something wasn't right. He seemed off—wired, upset, and wary. I could feel him assessing us, measuring how glad we were to see him. And he definitely didn't want to talk about his time in Germany.

The army was Jim's permanent home, even as his actual residences changed with each new assignment. He'd made a life for himself, but there was a sense that trouble was brewing, and within the family, we had questions we kept to ourselves. How was it, after eighteen years in the service, Jim had failed to advance beyond the level of staff sergeant? He'd always spoken of wanting to become an airborne helicopter pilot, or of joining the Special Forces, which had distinguished itself in the short-lived invasion of Grenada the previous year. But his career had seemed to flatline. His next post was as a drill instructor at Fort Hood, a respectable but middling job. It seemed to be an unmistakable fact: Jim's career wasn't moving forward. Instead, he seemed to be marching in place.

In addition, Jim's personal life was troubled. A few years after his last tour in Vietnam, during a three-year assignment at Fort Rucker, Alabama, Jim had met and married Amy, a bright and pretty dark-haired young woman a few years his junior.

When my parents met Amy, they liked her immediately, and they hoped that her easygoing, sparkly personality would have a positive effect on Jim. Amy soon gave birth to a daughter, Tracy, and Jim seemed to be reborn, not only a soldier now, but also a proud husband and father. My parents thought that a wife and child would settle Jim, and provide him with the stability of a home life.

Unfortunately, the marriage lasted less than two years. Jim let us know that it hadn't worked out, and that he'd moved back onto the base. Shortly after that, Amy called Mom. She told her she was sorry about the breakup, but she had had no choice. "I loved him, but he beat me," she finally admitted. "When he drank, he couldn't control it. I had to get out. I had to protect Tracy."

What could Mom say? She blurted out an apology, as if she were the one whose hand had been raised against Amy. She begged her to stay in touch, to keep sending pictures of that dear little girl. But there had been no further communication from Amy.

Mom always felt bad that she had never met Jim's daughter, but she still hoped to. She reasoned that people get divorced all the time, and they work out custody arrangements. She assumed that Jim had some interaction with Tracy. However, he hadn't mentioned his daughter, so after John's wedding, as we were relaxing back home, Mom lightly broached the subject. "How's Tracy?"

Jim shrugged. "Don't know."

"Do you talk to her?"

"Nope."

"Oh, that's a shame." Mom looked at Jim expectantly, waiting for more.

"Amy's new husband adopted her," he said tersely. "She's not mine anymore."

The news was shocking and heartbreaking all at once. Poor Jim. Loneliness, disappointment, scar upon scar beneath the carefully constructed facade of strength. I suspect that Amy didn't want her little girl to have anything to do with Jim, and Jim's compliance was probably based on financial considerations. He would have reasoned that child support was too costly for a child he'd rarely see.

Mom knew her son, and understood better than anyone his tremendous capacity for hurt and grievance, his craving for approval and love, so great she could never satisfy it. "I'm sorry," was all she said, eager to drop the subject. She didn't want to go there, but Jim bristled at her show of compassion.

"What do you care about my daughter?" he asked bitterly. "You don't even care about *me*." The mood in the room suddenly changed. Jim was on his feet, standing inches from Mom, dwarfing her, his fists in clenched balls.

"Jim, you know that's not true," she protested.

"Nobody in this goddamned family cares about nothing. I'll bet you wish I wasn't even here."

He swung around, stumbled, and then was out the door, revving up his car with an angry roar, and peeling off down the street.

The front door burst open at 9:30 that night, as we were sitting in the living room, watching television. Dad was dozing, the cat in his lap. Mom's head was nodding. We were all sated with the long day, tired and thinking about going to bed.

Jim's entrance shocked us awake. He stood in the doorway, drunk, defiant, and wild-eyed, his arm around a very young and scantily clad woman. I thought to myself, she's a prostitute, although that might have been unfair. Maybe she was just a girl, also very drunk, whom he'd picked up at Angie's Bar, a favorite local hangout down the hill from our parents' home. By the startled look on her face, as she focused on the scene before her, it was obvious that she hadn't expected to be introduced to a version of the Walton family that night.

"This is Gail," Jim slurred, moving into the room and pulling her by the hand along with him. There was an uncomfortable silence as we stared, and Jim shouted, "What, you can't even say hello to my friend?"

That's the thing about our family. We were all brought up to be very well-behaved. Politeness first. In spite of the wildly inappropriate nature of the moment, the utter wrongness of Jim bursting in like this, we dragged out our trusty manners and plastered on thin smiles. "Hello, Gail," Mom murmured softly. "Hello," I said.

"I promised Gail a drink," Jim said, heading for a cupboard where he'd stashed a fifth of Jack Daniels earlier in the day.

Dad had found his voice, his sense of propriety finally pushed to its limits. "No," he said, rising from his chair, the cat scurrying out of the room. "No. How dare you bring this . . . this young woman . . . there are children here. Just get out. Go on. Get out." Dad moved angrily toward Jim.

There was a long pause as Dad and Jim stood eye to eye. You could smell the booze radiating off of Jim as he tried to stand steady against his father. Finally, he reached out and pulled Gail toward the still open front door. "They don't want us here," he mumbled tightly, his face an angry scowl. He slammed the door behind him.

Jim returned to the house that night, many hours later, when we were all asleep, and he fell into bed. When he walked into the kitchen looking for coffee late the next morning, he seemed to remember none of what had occurred, and no one mentioned it.

By now we were in minefield mode, tiptoeing through an emotional jungle, carefully examining the terrain before taking our next step. But like invisible mines buried too deep for even the most eagle-eyed demolition experts, an alcoholic's fury will defy any attempt at caution. The day stretched ahead, with a family barbecue in the works, and it seemed inevitable that something would blow. How could it not?

For the first time during Jim's visit, there was a palpable fear that went far beyond the usual uneasiness. We'd never witnessed violence from Jim, although we knew he was capable of it, based on Amy's claim. And we were well aware that with eighteen years in the army under his belt, Jim was now a professional soldier for whom violence was possible. That's not to say that the army exclusively breeds men of violence. But it trains men to fight, and it trains men to kill. No matter how highly disciplined a soldier might be, how otherwise kind, alcohol changes the equation. Jim had been a different person, an alien being, when he'd brought that young girl into our family's home the night before. None of us knew what he was capable of now. He didn't seem like a brother. He didn't seem like a member of our family anymore. Instead, he was like a dangerous stranger.

So, yes, we were concerned that morning, even frightened. We worried that Jim might have a gun in his possession. We just didn't know what to expect.

In the midst of all the turmoil, the only ones who didn't see the dark potential looming were the children. It was a strange paradox: kids simply adored Jim, and he them. Boys, in particular, looked up to him, this real-life army man with his rows of ribbons and badges. The comfort he could not achieve around adults, with our judgments and prickly questions, was more easily achieved with the boys. So when my young son excitedly told me that Jim was taking him golfing that morning, I couldn't say no. Paul was just too thrilled—in fact, he still talks about that golfing jaunt to this day. It's his only memory of Uncle Jim.

Watching them go off together, my redheaded brother and my redheaded boy, I thought they could have been father and son. It was a nice scene, and I forced myself to relax. Jim was so careful with Paul, so respectful. I much preferred that he introduce him to golf clubs than to guns.

They returned in midafternoon, Paul full of stories about his first golf game. By that point, the house was crowded with our siblings and their families. The grill was smoking, and several people were squeezed into the kitchen, preparing potato salad and baked beans, talking loudly to be heard above the family roar. I was sitting at the kitchen table, chopping vegetables and listening to the baseball game on the radio. Paul ran outside to join his cousins in the yard. Jim grabbed a beer from the fridge and drained it in one long swallow, and then opened another as he sat down beside me and leaned back in the kitchen chair.

"So, Catherine," he said, his eyes shining as the beer began loosening him up. He got right into it. "I'll bet you love living in New York with all those hippies and Commies. Do you send that nice kid of yours to a good Commie school?"

Ordinarily, I would have laughed at such a ridiculous comment, but you didn't laugh at Jim. That was rule one.

"Well, it isn't quite like that," I answered smoothly. "We're just normal people in New York City—you know, working and living like everyone else. And I've never been a Commie."

"Oh, right," he barked. He reached out and opened another beer—his third in minutes—and stared at me with a long, hard gaze. The old grievances were still burning in his eyes. It might have been 1968 for all he knew. He had frozen the tableau in place, polishing it over the years as my own life and sensibilities had moved on from those days.

Jim leaned in close enough for me to smell the beer on his breath. "You know what I've never been able to understand?" he asked ominously.

"No, what?" I edged back in my chair.

"What the hell you were thinking. You're one cold bitch to be waving your peace signs around while your brother is dying over there." He went on in this vein through two more beers, his indignation rising.

Idiotically, I kept trying to respond as if we were having a rational debate, as if I could explain my political philosophy, as if I could change his mind about me, as if I could inspire an understanding that would cause him to say, "Oh, OK. Now I see."

The effort wore me out. Finally, I said, "Jim, forget about the past. Let's talk about now." My impatience with the old stories, my apparent indifference to his pain infuriated Jim. He yanked his pant leg up to show me a jagged scar. "What about this?" he shouted.

All I could think to say was, "That's terrible. But come on, Jim. It's been fifteen years."

He slammed a hand down hard on the table, and at the sound, the others in the kitchen swiveled to stare at us. Everyone froze in place. Here we go, I thought. Here we go.

Jim was on his feet, leaning over me, shouting, in a rage. "You think you're so fuckin' holy!" he screamed. "You people make me sick. We could get blown to fuckin' bits, but your life is so perfect, you don't even care. You don't even fuckin' care."

Mom was by his side, her hand on his arm. "Jim, calm down," she said, trying to soothe him. "Maybe you'd better take it easy on the beers."

He swung around—in retrospect, I'm sure he had no idea what he was doing, he was probably somewhere else far away in his mind—and shoved Mom hard. Time seemed to stop for a moment. It was an act so unthinkable, so egregious, that it stunned all of us. In a blur, I watched two of my brothers barrel into the kitchen and drag Jim out into the front yard. Dad rushed in from the grill, and when he saw Mom leaning against the counter, gasping, he followed his sons out, as mad as I'd ever seen him. When he reached the yard, my brothers were whaling at Jim like small boys in a schoolyard fight, fists flying everywhere and landing again and again. Dad stood over them, shaking with fury. "Stop it! Stop!" he shouted.

He stared down at Jim, lying in the grass. "Get out," he said. "Just leave."

Jim's eyes were watery with confusion, humiliation, and rejection. "Don't worry," he managed to say. "I know when I'm not wanted."

He got to his feet and walked unsteadily into the house, where he made a quick call. Moments later, he returned to the yard carrying a bag. None of us spoke as we watched him. A car pulled into our driveway with Gail, the young girl from the night before, behind the wheel. Jim got in beside her, slamming the door with extra force. Our last sight of Jim was a profile of his stony face, staring straight ahead as Gail backed out and drove away.

—

SIX

ALL THAT
YOU CAN'T BE

THEY MARCHED DOWN Pennsylvania Avenue in Washington, D.C., fifteen to twenty thousand strong. They were ragged and poor, their faces wearing the hollow look we have come to associate with the hunger and hopelessness of the Depression era. Those marching were the veterans of World War I. They bore the scars, physical and psychological, of a war in which they had survived for months on end in the muck and mire of rat-infested trenches. They had endured intense artillery fire that left many permanently shell-shocked. They had suffered the assault of mustard gas, which singed their lungs and eyes and left their nervous systems horribly damaged.

The only thing that kept them going through those horrific days and nights was the anticipation that one day they would be lifted from the trenches and returned to that shining city on a hill called home.

At first, it seemed as though that promise would be fulfilled. The nation welcomed them back, and in 1924, Congress passed legislation granting special compensation bonuses for the veterans' sacrifice, amounting to $1 a day for domestic service, up to $500; and $1.25 a day for overseas service, up to $625. Certificates were granted to 3.5 million servicemen, set to mature in 1945.

But the Great Depression changed everything. Now they had been forced by circumstance to march once again. In May 1932, the soldiers arrived in Washington, D.C., hats in hand, to plead with Congress for an advance on the promised compensation. They were there to support a bill put forth by Texas congressman John Patman, calling for the immediate payment of World War I bonuses to rescue the livelihoods of those who had served. They traveled to the nation's capital by any means necessary—in empty railroad cars, on the backs of trucks, hitchhiking, driving, and on foot. They came because they were unemployed, poor, and hungry, and because Washington, D.C., was their last, desperate stop before complete destitution. They poured into the city day after day, with their wives, children, and friends in tow, setting up shanty towns in the swampy Anacostia Flats, just across the Anacostia River from the Capitol.

They called themselves the Bonus Expeditionary Force but came to be known as the Bonus Army. The people of Washington, in recognition of their service in the Great War, collected food and necessities, and helped them build the makeshift camps.

But at the Department of the Army, Chief of Staff Douglas MacArthur looked on in dismay, convinced that the catalysts of the march were not legitimate veterans, but Communist organizers. He made his case to President Herbert Hoover, who was facing an uphill reelection bid that year.

Hoover, seeking a way out of a public relations nightmare, allowed himself to be persuaded that the Bonus Army was not only organized and promoted by Communists, but was also fueled by Democratic Party instigators seeking to embarrass him. As the Bonus Army marched down Pennsylvania Avenue and in front of the White House each day, Hoover huddled with congressional leaders, urging them to override Patman's bill.

On June 15, the House of Representatives passed Patman's measure, and briefly, the thrill of victory wafted through the air.

But two days later, the Senate overwhelmingly defeated the bill, by a vote of 62–18. It bears noting that President Hoover was not in town for the vote. He was in Chicago, accepting the nomination of the Republican Party for a second term as president. Nowhere in his lengthy, detailed address to the convention did Hoover mention the plight of the veterans, much less the many thousands gathered at the Capitol. Upon his return to Washington, Hoover ordered the Bonus Army to disperse. Congress had spoken, and he urged them to pack up their tents and return to their homes, where they were free to scrape by any way that they could. Many left, but about ten thousand veterans refused to go. For more than a month, they continued to live in the shantytowns and march by the thousands down Pennsylvania Avenue, reasserting their demands.

At midday on July 28, 1932, an amazing sight on Pennsylvania Avenue drew hundreds of government workers out of their offices.

Douglas MacArthur himself was standing at the head of a military contingent of six hundred fully armed soldiers. Five tanks rolled down the street at their rear, their clanking treads and swiveling gun turrets announcing their incongruous purpose. The reality dawned on the shocked bystanders: The United States government was preparing to launch an attack on its own veterans.

As the crowds roared, "Shame! Shame!" MacArthur's forces, led by Major George Patton and Major Dwight D. Eisenhower, advanced on the Bonus Army, driving them back across the river to their camps, injuring many, and enveloping the entire area in the choking fumes of tear gas. By sheer force of arms, they drove the Bonus Army out of town, and then set fire to their camps. The death toll was relatively minor—two men killed by troops, two infants asphyxiated by tear gas—but the moral toll was far greater. It was vast and unforgettable.

The following day, President Hoover announced, "A challenge to the authority of the United States Government has been met, swiftly and firmly.

"After months of patient indulgence, the Government met overt lawlessness as it always must be met if the cherished processes of self-government are to be preserved. We cannot tolerate the abuse of Constitutional rights by those who would destroy all government, no matter who they may be. Government cannot be coerced by mob rule."

Later, Hoover would respond to a congressional investigation by arguing that the marchers were Communists, outlaws, and troublemakers in veterans' clothing, further slandering the brave men who simply wanted the money they had been promised. The Bonus Army was the final nail in Hoover's presidential coffin. Later that year, he was defeated by Franklin D. Roosevelt.

The story of the Bonus Army is instructive on two counts. First, it demonstrates a historical pattern of broken promises to military veterans. But the Bonus Army also has a positive legacy. It triggered action in the next war, including the adoption of the GI Bill of Rights in 1944. The GI Bill, which provided small-business loans, low-interest mortgages, education payments, and other benefits to veterans, is largely credited with putting World War II veterans back on their feet. During the GI Bill's first decade, more than 280,000 farm and small-business loans were granted to veterans of World War II and the Korean War. The bill was eliminated in 1973, just as the Vietnam War was winding down. For a time, the Small Business Administration had a special loan program for Vietnam veterans, but by the mid-1990s, it was phased out as well.

But never fear! To all those starry-eyed, strapped-for-cash, minimally skilled young men and women out there in America, the military has a deal for you. A twenty-first-century bonus army, but this time with cash on the line.

Enlistment bonuses are a longtime military tradition, but with the need for replacement troops in Iraq and Afghanistan reaching desperate levels, the pot got sweetened in 2007. Any army recruit willing to ship out immediately would receive a hefty cash bonus—$10,000 upon completion of basic training and advanced individual training, and $10,000 more spread over the remaining period of service, usually three years.

Within three weeks of announcing the lucrative "quick ship" bonus in July 2007, the army had signed up more than four thousand new recruits. Ninety-two percent said that the money closed the deal for them.

The Department of Defense was pretty strict about the rules governing the payment of these bonuses. If soldiers failed to serve out their full term of enlistment, they couldn't collect. Fair enough. The military was protecting its interests, making sure that contractual agreements were upheld. Twenty grand is a big chunk of change.

In the beginning, no one was asking the obvious question: what if a soldier suffered combat injuries that made it impossible to serve the full enlistment period? Everyone assumed that the rule wouldn't apply in those cases. It didn't take long, however, for that assumption to be dashed, as reports of grievously wounded soldiers who had been shipped home and discharged from the military began to reach the public. Time and again, these soldiers, who had made extreme sacrifices that would leave them crippled and scarred for the rest of their lives, were being asked to return thousands of dollars in bonus money.

In late 2007, former Army Private First Class Jordan Fox became the public face of the despicable fine print of the signing-bonus giveback. While serving in Iraq, Fox was injured by a roadside bomb. He suffered a serious back injury, and he lost the sight in his right eye. No longer battle-ready, Fox was honorably discharged from the army.

A few weeks after his discharge, a letter came in the mail from the Defense Department. Expecting to find the "thanks of a grateful nation," Fox opened the letter and found instead a bill for $3,000. The army wanted part of the enlistment bonus back.

It wasn't just the strain of coming up with the cash that upset Fox. It was the slap in the face, the absence of any gratitude. "I tried to do my best and serve my country. I was unfortunately hurt in the process," he said. "Now they're telling me they want their money back."

A signing bonus is a gamble on the future, and even the NFL does not recoup signing-bonus money when a player is injured in a football game. But the military—arguably the riskiest arena of all—was calling foul against its injured warriors.

A familiar drama ensued. The Department of Defense expressed embarrassment. Congress expressed outrage. A flurry of newspaper articles kept the outrage roiling for a couple of weeks before the media turned its attention elsewhere. But would anything come of it?

The matter was first addressed by the bipartisan Commission on Care for America's Returning Wounded Warriors, co-chaired by former senator Bob Dole and former secretary of health and human services Donna Shalala. The commission contacted the Department of Defense and was assured that the bonuses would be paid to soldiers wounded at war. That assurance was enough to satisfy Dole and Shalala, who didn't even mention the issue in the commission's final report. However, there was no hard data about how many soldiers might have been shortchanged and whether or not the situation could arise again in the future.

In Congress, Representative Jason Altmire introduced the Veterans Guaranteed Bonus Act to formally ensure that wounded veterans were paid the entirety of any signing bonus they had been promised within thirty days after discharge for combat-related wounds. The legislation passed the House, but as of this writing, it is still under consideration by the Senate.

The Department of Defense insisted all along that the rule about returning bonuses wasn't supposed to apply to wounded soldiers. But this public stance failed to explain why so many of them had been asked to return the money.

Sure, the bonus army ruckus might just be an example of incompetence, a case of the left hand not knowing what the right hand was doing. But it also exposes a common dilemma our wounded warriors face—the tendency to pile on insults until embarrassed policymakers cry uncle and are forced to make big public concessions. In the midst of this exhausting process, many soldiers have their spirits broken. By the time public officials start saying, "Mistakes were made," it's usually too late to undo the damage to the early victims.

In his 2002 memoir, *Worth the Fighting For*, John McCain wrote of those who fought in the Vietnam War, "Their heroism was a beautiful fatalism. They stayed loyal to a doomed cause. But their salvation was found in the ultimate discovery that they had not sacrificed vainly, that they had died for something else, something greater."

Many weary veterans of that war might have cause to ask what greater purpose their "beautiful fatalism" gained them— beyond the vague idealism of empty rhetoric. Today's fighting forces might well ask the same. The charge to support the troops becomes little more than a cynical slogan when it is clear that the government is working overtime to cut their pay and benefits. Since the beginning of the war in Iraq, there have been cuts every year in the veterans' budget. The Bush administration's 2009 budget contained these items:

- A proposed cut in pay for 148,000 troops serving in Iraq.
- A rise in prescription drug costs for veterans that would add a $250 enrollment fee and increase the co-pay amount from $7 to $15 for veterans earning over $24,000 a year.
- The elimination of health-care benefits for 160,000 middle-income veterans earning more than $25,000 a year.
- A 50 percent cut in funding for research and treatment of brain injuries caused by bomb blasts—traumatic brain injury being the most common and significant injury in Iraq; and funding cuts for prosthetic research and development—loss of limbs caused by improvised explosive devices (IEDs), the second most common and significant injury in Iraq.
- A cut in funding for hiring claims processors. This item is especially galling in light of the 400,000- to 600,000-person backlog in processing claims. Injured soldiers on average spend six to eight months waiting to receive any disability pay.

The Bush administration also opposed legislation that would provide full benefits to reservists and National Guardsmen serving in Iraq, even though their tours were extended for up to two years. Twenty percent of our military has no health coverage at all.

The cold calculations of the budget contrast sharply with the heat of the rhetoric, and they present a practical problem for soldiers already having a hard time making ends meet. Even as their loved ones are engaged in wars in Iraq and Afghanistan, military families struggle to get by at home. The lower ranks of the military are filled with the working poor—young men and women from economically depressed areas for whom the military represents the only viable opportunity for higher education and a stable career. According to the Pentagon's own statistics, 40 percent of military families face "substantial financial difficulties." The majority of enlisted soldiers take home about $1,300 a month before taxes, a tough stretch for a family with children.

Brandeis University's Center on Hunger and Poverty reports that up to one-half of military families need food stamps and welfare support, giving lie to the myth that the military takes care of its own. Poverty and hunger have become so common among families of deployed troops that the international aid organization Feed the Children has developed a special program to offer them relief. For two years running, the organization, whose primary mission is to help Third World nations, has delivered nearly one million pounds of food to more than ten thousand families at twelve military bases in the United States. Food kitchens from California to Texas to New Jersey have reported a sharp increase in the number of military families seeking their help.

According to Barbara Ehrenreich, whose book *Nickel and Dimed* exposed the plight of the working poor, military families are so stretched for money that the army now includes food stamp applications in its orientation packets for new recruits. "Market forces ensure that a volunteer army will necessarily be an army of the poor," Ehrenreich writes. "The trouble is, enlistment does not do a whole lot to brighten one's economic outlook. Frontline battle troops, most of whom have been in the military for about a year, earn less than $16,000 a year—which puts them at about the level of theater ushers and Walmart clerks. Even second lieutenants, at a starting salary of $26,000 a year, earn less than pest control workers and shoe repairers."

According to a calculation by the U.S. Census Bureau, a family of four people, including two children under age eighteen, earning an annual income of $17,463 or less, lives at the poverty level. Many military families don't even meet this subsistence-level standard.

Even at higher ranks, the pay is paltry. An army or Marine Corps sergeant averages around $27,000 a year; if he or she is in a combat zone, there's an additional $225 a month, for a grand total of $28,700 a year.

When I visited Killeen, Texas, I found that the number of homeless veterans and veterans seeking help at soup kitchens has spiked noticeably in the last two years. Killeen, where my brother lived and died, is the home of Fort Hood, the largest military installation in the United States. Base families are the new underclass, and it shows every sign of becoming entrenched. Here's the bottom line: stay in the military and you'll be poor; return to civilian life and you'll be poor.

Visiting some of these families, I was struck by the seemingly disproportionate numbers of African Americans and Latinos in the lower ranks, an impression confirmed by the statistics. While blacks make up about 12 percent of the U.S. population, they comprise 22 percent of the military. Half of the enlisted women in the military are black. Together, blacks and Latinos account for more than one-third of the casualties in the Iraq War. Blacks and Latinos tend to get the grunt work. They are heavily concentrated in service jobs and the infantry, but practically nonexistent in the more desirable roles as military pilots or in Special Forces units.

We're all familiar with the army's recruitment campaign, whose old slogan, "Be all that you can be," held the promise of future earnings as a trained professional. The idea that the military is an ideal place to learn skills that give you a leg up in the civilian world has been a successful marketing tool. It is also a myth.

A 2007 study by Abt Associates found that 18 percent of veterans who seek jobs are still unemployed three years after discharge from the military, while one in four who manage to find employment earn less than $21,840 a year. Veterans earn an average of 20 percent less than nonveterans. The study states that employers often believe negative stereotypes about what kind of employees veterans will be. They report fears that vets will be too rigid, lack education, or suffer from PTSD that might impair their performance. Sure, they *want* to support the returning soldiers, they really do. But business is business, ya know?

Recent studies also show that the skills acquired in the military are almost never transferable to civilian life. The training soldiers receive—even the technical skills shown on television commercials—is usually specific to the military. In a recent Ohio State study, only 12 percent of male veterans and 6 percent of female veterans surveyed made *any* use of the skills they learned in the military in their civilian jobs. A 2007 survey by Monster.com, the online job recruitment site, found that 81 percent of returning military veterans did not feel fully prepared to enter the workforce. Of those, 76 percent felt unable to translate their military skills to the civilian world.

While active military and veterans alike find themselves nickel and dimed by the bureaucracy charged with their care, it was leaked in 2007 that hefty performance bonuses, totaling $3.8 million, were paid to officials at the VA that year. Secretary of Veterans Affairs Jim Nicholson defended the practice, saying it was necessary to retain good employees. But, given the failure of the VA to efficiently handle hundreds of thousands of backlogged claims, one wonders how he defines performance.

Jim Webb, the junior senator from Virginia, is a flamboyant redhead who will never be anointed diplomat of the year. Weeks after his election, at a reception President George W. Bush hosted to welcome new members, Webb got in the president's face right off the bat. When Bush, in a friendly manner, asked Webb how his son, a marine lance corporal serving in Iraq, was doing,

Webb sharply replied that what he really wanted was to see his son brought back home. Bush responded testily, "I didn't ask you that, I asked how he's doing."

Webb later said he was so angry that he wanted to punch Bush. Fortunately, he held his fire. But fire is a trademark of Webb's style. A highly decorated marine in Vietnam, who later served as the youngest secretary of the navy during the Reagan administration, Webb has always been a passionate advocate for soldiers and veterans. He is also a prolific novelist, whose vivid prose is often blush-worthy. His rocky marital history includes three wives. But there is one indisputable fact about James Webb: soldiers love him.

The United States Senate operates on a code of seniority, and new senators are expected to ease themselves in, to essentially be seen and not heard until they learn the ropes. But on his first day in office, Webb introduced an ambitious piece of legislation titled The Twenty-First Century GI Bill. Webb's bill outlined benefits that would be available to all members of the military who have served on active duty since September 11, 2001. It included re-servists and National Guard members, who typically received only a fraction of the benefits available to active-duty troops. Eligible veterans would receive education benefits equaling the highest tuition rate of the most expensive in-state public college or university, and they would be provided a monthly stipend for housing determined by geographical area. Beyond that, Webb's bill would create a program in which the government would provide a dollar-for-dollar match to contributions from private educational institutions with higher tuition rates than those covered under the bill. Veterans would also have fifteen years to use their educational assistance, compared to ten years under the current law. Webb pointed out that his bill, projected to cost about $2.5 billion per year, was roughly equivalent to the cost of operations in Iraq for less than a week.

The Defense Department and the White House fought back, claiming that Webb's bill was so generous that it would discourage soldiers from reenlisting and thus seriously deplete the volunteer military. In testimony before Congress, a Defense Department official assured public officials that "the current program for active duty is basically sound and serves its purpose in support of the all-volunteer force. The department finds no need for the kind of sweeping—and expensive—changes offered."

Senator John McCain was one former sailor who might have been expected to wholeheartedly support Webb's bill. However, on the campaign trail in his run for the presidency, McCain, the self-appointed "maverick," echoed the administration's concerns about troop retention, and he vowed to oppose Webb's bill. He also petulantly complained that he would have been more than willing to negotiate a better bill with his "good friend" Jim Webb, but sadly, Webb's office wasn't interested in a discussion.

"He's so full of it," Webb roared. "I have personally talked to John three times. I made a personal call to [McCain aide] Mark Salter months ago asking that they look at this."

In spite of stiff opposition, Webb would not back down. "These are the people who answered the call," he argued. "These are the people who moved willingly forward toward the sound of the guns."

As the vote on Webb's bill approached, President Bush announced his intention to veto it if it passed. But the momentum was growing in the bill's favor as senators and congressmen heard from their constituents. The people of America wanted to compensate their fighting forces.

On May 15, 2008, the GI Bill passed the House of Representatives by a vote of 266–156. On May 22, the U.S. Senate followed suit, approving the bill by a veto-proof margin of 75–22. Senator John McCain was not present for the vote.

Having little choice but to sign the bill, President Bush put a good face on it. At the signing he declared, "The bill is a result of close collaboration between my administration and members of both parties on Capitol Hill . . . I want to thank members who worked hard for the GI Bill expansion, especially Senators Webb, Warner, Graham, Burr, and McCain. This bill shows that even in an election year, Democrats and Republicans can come together to stand behind our troops."

Webb watched with a smile. Never mind that three of the senators mentioned—Graham, Burr, and McCain—had opposed the bill. Never mind that McCain had withheld his vote. That was politics, and he could shrug it off. He was satisfied. He got what he wanted.

Now all they had to do was make it work.

It should surprise no one that military families have been vulnerable to the latest scourge of the underclass, subprime mortgages. Indeed, they were considered frontline targets during the subprime boom. Here was a population that moved frequently, was paid little, and often had bad credit that made it impossible to get conventional loans. Many were lured by the promise of home ownership, the chance to have a stake in the economy they had fought to preserve. Sadly, their piece of the American dream was a defective one.

According to Danielle Babb, a real estate and economics expert who teaches at the University of California–Irvine, foreclosures have affected military families over others by a four-to-one ratio. Babb studied foreclosure filings in ten cities and towns within ten miles of military bases across the country during the first half of 2007, when the foreclosure crisis was just beginning to hit. She found that foreclosure filings rose 217 percent, while the national average for the same period was 59 percent.

Among the top "surge areas" of foreclosures, she said, was Columbia, South Carolina, home to Fort Jackson, where the rate rose 492 percent in the first quarter of 2007. Coming in second was Woodbridge, Virginia, near Marine Corps Base Quantico, where foreclosure filings went up 414 percent.

In addition, foreclosures tripled in communities surrounding Norfolk Naval Base, Virginia, and Camp Pendleton, California. They more than doubled in Havelock, North Carolina, home to Marine Corps Air Station Cherry Point.

There is an obvious reason for the problem. Military families were especially attracted to adjustable rate mortgages, since frequent moves required by military life made it likely that they would have to sell their homes before the rates jumped. But suddenly those families found the values of their homes plummeting to a point where they owed more than their properties were worth.

In this arena, Congress and the White House did cooperate, quickly passing and signing into law the Foreclosure Prevention Act of 2008. Among other things, the bill protects those serving overseas from foreclosures while they are away, and it extends the length of time banks must wait to start foreclosure proceedings upon a soldier's return from combat. But these are Band-Aid fixes to a far worse crisis.

The housing market collapse raises the specter of homelessness, which is all too real for veterans. Although accurate numbers are impossible to come by (no one keeps national records on homeless veterans), the VA estimates that nearly 200,000 veterans are homeless on any given night, and nearly 400,000 experience homelessness over the course of a year. Conservatively, one out of every three homeless men (they're mostly men) sleeping in a doorway, alley, or cardboard box in our cities and rural communities has worn a uniform and served this country.

This tragic fact was raised early in the 2008 presidential primary by John Edwards, who, in spite of his well-documented sins, cared deeply about the plight of the poor. Edwards spoke movingly of the "two hundred thousand veterans who go to sleep on grates and under bridges." Many veterans groups were encouraged to hear the issue brought front and center in a presidential campaign; for all the rhetoric about supporting the troops, veterans issues rarely come up during presidential elections, even when the candidates themselves (John Kerry, John McCain) are running on their military biographies.

Enter Bill O'Reilly, the tempestuous right-wing host of *The O'Reilly Factor*. He mocked John Edwards's sentiment and statistics, and made the search for homeless veterans a centerpiece of several of his shows. "We're still looking for all the veterans sleeping under the bridges," he cackled, as if it were a joke. "If anyone finds them, let us know." O'Reilly ultimately concluded that "there are a few, but they're either mentally ill or addicted." End of story.

Where does one even begin to address this level of ignorance and cruelty? Some veterans offered to take O'Reilly on a tour, but I guess he didn't accept. It was easier to spread poison and watch his ratings rise.

I met Pete in a local soup kitchen. He served in Vietnam, and has been homeless off and on since 1979, jailed twice for gun violations. "In the army, you got a problem, you got a gun," he says with a shrug. "I came back home, and I had to be armed. I slept with a pistol. I'd pull a gun if a guy looked at my wife funny. She ain't my wife no more." A heroin addict, Pete lives on the streets where his closest friends are also veterans.

I met Carl, who was easy to spot because of his heavily patched fatigue jacket, with "MIA-POW" stitched into the fabric. Carl was not an addict. He'd just had a hard time "getting it together" since the Gulf War and was intermittently homeless. I asked Carl why he wasn't receiving benefits from the army. Surely he was entitled. He shrugged. "I don't know anything about that," he said.

By some estimates, there are more than two million physically and mentally disabled veterans and their widows who are entitled to benefits they haven't claimed. Often, they aren't even aware they *can* claim them. Meeting fragile souls like Pete and Carl, I can well imagine that the requirements of the claims process—lengthy forms, phone calls, appeals—are just too overwhelming. They can't handle it, and so they accept their fates.

In June 2008, the plight of disenfranchised veterans struck close to home when the remains of Robert Hewett, a fifty-seven-year-old homeless Vietnam veteran, were found in the woods behind a shopping center near where I live. The cause of death was homicide. He had been beaten to death.

Hewett had been living in the woods for fifteen years, a victim of a crushing despair. The trigger for his emotional collapse was the death of his seven-year-old son from cancer—a death he was convinced was related to his exposure to Agent Orange in Vietnam. Unable to cope with the guilt and loss, Hewett retreated from life, living out his penance in isolation. He was buried with full military honors in a moving funeral ceremony conducted by the Marine Corps League. More than one hundred people showed up to send Hewett off. None of the friends, families, and strangers who attended had been able to save him while he was alive. Giving him a death with dignity was small comfort.

Another army slogan came to mind when I spoke with homeless veterans: "An Army of One." Meant to depict strength, initiative, and individual achievement, it was abandoned in 2006 in favor of "Army Strong." Maybe it was just too hard to evoke patriotism with the old words, given the isolation of so many veterans, who feel as if they are, indeed, an army of one.

SEVEN

———

BROTHER LOST

1985

I'VE NEVER KNOWN a grudge to take hold in my family. Tempers might flare, but we always make up. We can fight about politics, religion—you name it—but the next day dawns with a cheery let-bygones-be-bygones air. An apology, sealed with a joke and a hug, and all is well.

With Jim, it was a little tougher. Everyone understood that when Dad told him to leave, it wasn't supposed to be forever. We all assumed he would return, and we wanted him to, just as long as he left his demons at the door.

"Why doesn't someone help him?" Mom asked, again and again. She meant the army, of course. Maybe it was too easy to place blame with the army, but it was also a fair question. Jim's whole life was the army, and his troubles were plain to see. He was losing his grip.

The truth is, the army of the sixties, seventies, and eighties was a drinking culture. I've spoken to many veterans who served during those decades, and for some of them, their clearest memories were of hanging out at the makeshift canteens in Vietnam, or at the officers' clubs, or in civilian bars. Their fond recollections of drinking buddies blurred with those of fighting buddies, becoming almost indistinguishable.

115

My brother Greg, who served in the navy and remembers the twenty-five-cent martinis at the enlisted men's club, made the observation that "the dominant culture in the military is sex and booze. In this rough and rugged male institution, many of the people in leadership, particularly the enlisted leaders, glorify hard drinking, hard living, and sex with any woman available, whether or not you have to pay for her. It's always been this way and it always will be in the hard-charging military environment. It's very easy for me to see how Jim would have been swept up and participated in this culture, particularly the drinking."

But alcohol is much more than a social lubricant. It is also a means of forgetting, a way to calm nerves that don't stop jittering and effect a bravado that ordinary life cannot summon. According to William Schlenger, a psychologist who was a principal investigator for the National Vietnam Veterans' Readjustment Study (NVVRS), alcohol abuse, post-traumatic stress disorder, and depression comprise an "unholy trinity" for some soldiers in the wake of combat. But his study confirmed that alcohol was the real demon. Overall, Vietnam veterans did not have higher rates of drug abuse than the general population. But they did have a level of problem drinking much higher than nonveterans or even veterans of prior wars. After factoring in demographic variables, such as upbringing, education levels, and social status, the NVVRS concluded that alcohol abuse was a direct outcome of the Vietnam experience, not prewar experiences.

I could see those signs in Jim's demeanor and behavior. But he was not a veteran outside the scope of the military's oversight. He was a staff sergeant at a major army base, showing up for work every day. Did they not see? Wasn't there a system in place for insisting that soldiers get psychological or substance abuse aid when they clearly needed it?

SOLDIER When Jim put on his uniform, he was transformed from a troubled youth to a man of dignity. He loved his uniform, and wore it as a
shield to mask his personal struggles.

THE GREAT WAR My maternal grandfather, Walter McArtor, lied about his age and joined the army at age seventeen, as the United States entered World War I. He was part of the 63rd Artillery, shipped out from Puget Sound to the muddy trenches of France. He died in 1966, and was buried the day Jim left Seattle for army basic training.

MY FATHER'S SHIP In World War II, my father sailed to the South Pacific on the original USS *Kitty Hawk*, and participated in the Battle of Midway. A photo of his ship hung on the wall of our living room, although Dad rarely spoke of his war experiences.

GOOD TIMES My parents met after World War II. They were a beautiful, hopeful couple. The sacrifices and hardships of war were packed away in an old cedar chest, along with Dad's uniform.

THE VANGUARD Greg, Jim, and I were the first of our parents' nine children. As our mother recalls, "Jim was the bravest kid I ever knew." But sandwiched in the lineup between his smart older brother and his adored younger sister, Jim struggled to find his place in the world.

HONK For more than six years, vying groups of protesters have stood on opposite corners of Route 59 in Rockland County, urging motorists to "Honk for peace" or "Honk to support the troops." I've driven past them hundreds of times, wondering why we can't do both.

MARCHING This anti-war protest, organized by students at the University of Washington, shut down Seattle's I-5 freeway. I was there, to the dismay of my parents.

THE FINAL TOUR In 1971, Jim served his third and final tour in Vietnam, with the 815th Engineer Battalion. By then, the tone of the battlefront had changed—as evidenced by the love beads.

ENGINEER'S PRIDE Jungle clearing was an essential function of the engineer divisions in Vietnam. Believe it or not, this massive dozer, driven by John Walker of the 87th Engineer Battalion, was dropped into the field by a Skycrane helicopter. Today, Walker hosts a Web site for my brother's old battalion, and is instrumental in keeping the memories alive.

VALOR Barely a month into his second tour in Vietnam, with the 87th Engineer Battalion, Jim was wounded in action and received a Purple Heart. His injury was not severe, and he soon returned to the field.

A FATEFUL GATHERING The last time the nine of us were together, in 1984, we looked happy and close. But events that weekend created a permanent rift in our relationship with Jim. (*left to right*) John, Paul, Catherine, Mary, Greg, Margaret, Jim; (*front*) Joanne, Tom.

BROTHERHOOD William L. Smith, a former gun pilot with the 129th Assault Helicopter Company in Vietnam, and now a veteran living in Texas, was Jim's friend until the end. He was compassionate about Jim's problems. "Vietnam left many scars on all of us," Bill said. "They were not necessarily physical scars, but psychological scars."

A BEACON Every Memorial Day, watch fires light up the sky along the Hudson River. Tended by veterans, they serve as a token of solidarity with the lost patrols that never returned.

IN MEMORY Each year, on Memorial Day weekend, Rolling Thunder holds a massive motorcycle rally in Washington, D.C. In 2008, more than 400,000 veterans participated in memory of the war heroes who never came home.

HERO GRUNTS Jay Hirsch, a Vietnam veteran who took this picture, describes The Three Servicemen statue in Washington D.C. this way: "The statute represents the camaraderie and the closeness of the grunt. Not Anglo, African, Hispanic or Native American, but flesh, bone and blood! They all shared everything and they all bleed the same color . . . their job for their Country and Flag."

NEVER FORGET "Real men cry," says photographer, Jay Hirsch. Every day at The Wall, veterans weep for their lost brothers and their own lost promise.

Jim was the kind of guy who would have to be ordered to seek help. He'd have considered it a pansy act to request it for himself. Furthermore, in the case of addiction, the addicted person is the last to recognize the problem. So Mom's was a legitimate question: where was the army?

A few weeks after Jim left home in the wake of his disastrous explosion, Mom sat down and wrote him a letter. She told him she was sorry about the way his visit went. She told him that she loved him. She gently broached the subject of his getting help for his drinking. She reassured him that the whole family was behind him. She asked him to write or call collect, or to send a phone number so she could call him. I know my mother. She is a wonderful letter writer, able to spread warmth across the page along with her flowing script. It should have soothed Jim's nerves a bit, calmed him down, convinced him that all would be well. It wasn't the first time there had been conflicts between my parents and Jim. They had come through them in the past. Surely they would again.

There was no response to Mom's letter.

At Christmas, Mom sent her usual package, carefully wrapping small items that she knew Jim would enjoy, enclosing a loving card and some recent family photos. Again, she urged him to write or call, to let everyone know how he was doing.

Again, no response.

Her third letter was returned, addressee unknown. Jim was lost. Somewhere in Texas. He wasn't *really* lost, of course. We could have tracked him down through the army, but no one wanted to jump into that fray—not yet, at least.

Then one day he phoned, and he sounded terrible. Mom thought he might be crying. "Something happened," he told her. "I may not be able to talk to you for a while."

"Jim, tell me," she urged him.

He would say only that there had been a car accident, but he was OK. "Don't worry, Mom," he said. "I'll talk to you soon."

And then he dropped out of touch, and another year went by before we heard from him. We speculated endlessly. Maybe he'd been drunk and had a bad car accident—plausible enough. Maybe he'd killed someone. Maybe he was in jail.

Finally, on Mother's Day 1986, a large, flowery card arrived, with a note inside:

Dear Mom,

Good news! I'm retiring. Twenty years is enough for me. I'll be getting some kind of job, and I'll have plenty of time for golf. I'm looking forward to that.

Mom, I wish I could be there on Mother's Day, but I promise to make it up there soon. Give my love to everyone and tell them I miss them.

Love,

Jim

There was, at last, a return address on the envelope. Peace was restored. Jim had been lost and now he was found. But my parents had a fresh worry. Retirement at the age of thirty-seven didn't seem like something Jim would welcome. He loved the military, and he was still young enough to advance. He hadn't held a civilian job since he was in high school. Could he make it on his own?

We bandied the subject around in family discussions that went something like this:

"He's young. He's strong."

"Yeah, but the drinking . . ."
"Maybe he's over that."
"Hmmm . . ."
"He'll have a military pension."
"And PX privileges at Fort Hood."
"But what will he *do*?"

That was the question that concerned us the most. Jim's identity was completely fused with his army pride. Who would he be now? And why, really, was he retiring? The Jim we knew wouldn't retire—would he? Unless he had to.

We decided to take a wait-and-see approach. Wait to hear the details, and then see how worried we should be. But Jim's rare letters to Mom and Dad, though warm, were maddeningly short on information. We wanted to know about his life, but instead, he wrote nostalgically about Seattle, about coming home, about wishing he was there.

> It has really been hot here for the last couple of months. It's been so long since I have seen rain, it makes me wish I was in Seattle right now.

> How about those Mariners! I finally have something to brag about to all these Texas Ranger fans.

His letters always ended the same way:

> Well, I'm going to let you go now . . .

It was haunting. *I'm going to let you go.* In fact, Jim surely felt that we were the ones who had let *him* go. Sometimes he promised to visit, but he never did. Every so often he would call collect and ask our parents if they could spare a little money. The figure was always small and always very specific—$149 or $183. These requests perplexed our parents because they seemed desperate, and indicated that Jim wasn't doing well, in spite of his pension and his assurances that he had a job. Dad was peeved and Mom was hurt that Jim never called for any other reason. They always sent the money, though. They always urged him to come home.

"*This* is my home," he replied.

The years rolled by. Our family changed. Now our parents were alone in their house, their children raised and leading lives of their own. Most of them remained in Seattle, and the number of grandchildren grew. Dad was forced to retire when his company closed. As I mentioned earlier, retirement was not kind to our father. He'd worked for the same company for thirty-five years, striding out the door at 6:30 A.M. each day, creating a life and a semblance of community around his job. He was a company man through and through, rising up the ranks at Foremost Dairies, from a milkman to a sales executive. Dad was an extremely likeable guy, warm and funny, a loyal friend, and a tireless worker. He enjoyed being around people from all walks of life, and was energized by his associations. Retirement felt like a lonely exile to him. Even though he got involved at the hospital and church, and put his artistic skills to work making signs for local supermarkets ("What a peach! $1.49/lb."), the absence of a regular schedule threw him for a loop. Mom was working full-time, and often he was home alone with the cat.

Dad had never been sick a day in his life, so when he became severely ill with liver problems, it was a great shock to everyone. In the years after his diagnosis, we watched our strapping father shrink and grow thin. His humor became more forced, and his bright blue eyes dulled.

A few months before he died, Dad called me in New York. "I need you to do me a favor," he said.

"Sure."

"I want to find an old navy buddy. He lives in New Jersey, or at least that's where he was from. Since you're back there, maybe you could find him for me."

"I don't know," I said. "New Jersey's a big place."

"Just try," he said, and gave me the name.

I didn't try very hard, and I never found Dad's buddy. I am certain that if he were to make the same request today, I would pull out all the stops. Then, I didn't understand how deeply important it was to him, how much he needed that connection. Maybe it would have given him some comfort as he faced his final days. I won't dwell on my regret, except to say that, like so many civilians, I never appreciated the existential bond between military comrades, a bond that could survive a lifetime. Now I know better. I have seen how men who went their separate ways after a war can reunite forty years later and pick up where they left off, comfortably lapsing into the familiar lingo, the certain knowledge of each other. The desire of an older man to connect with a military buddy is nothing like the casual interest one might have in looking up a high-school teammate or a college friend. Those ties are broken with ease; the military tie is never broken.

Dad's death, when it came in 1996, rocked our family. What would we do without him? How could we put him in the ground? Mom was strong, but she wanted her children around her—all of them. So the most urgent matter was how to reach Jim, and this was no small task. Although we had an address, we had no phone number or any other method of contacting him in an emergency. We tried Fort Hood. We tried sending a telegram. Nothing worked. I think that was when we truly realized how far away Jim was. We agreed that it would break Jim's heart that he wasn't there to bury his father, but so be it.

At Dad's funeral, it was left to our brother Greg, the eldest, to deliver a eulogy. His words were a beautiful tribute, spoken through a haze of tears. Looking down at the flag-draped coffin, Greg spoke of our patriot father:

> When President Franklin Roosevelt asked for support in the war effort, I think Dad was one of the first to report to the recruiting station. The fact that he was part of this national effort to win a great victory for democracy and civilization was always important to him. Even though he had served in one of the coldest, bitterest regions, Dad always had a great love for the sea and for the navy. He sometimes regretted not continuing on to retirement in the navy. The years in military service translated into lifelong loyalty to the country and concern about its future. Dad was a good American citizen; he never missed a vote. He did not like to discuss politics, but there was no doubt about his feelings toward this country. The American flag was prominently on display outside our home, and not just on holidays.

Greg understood that although Dad was always defined by his civilian roles—family, work, and church—his grounding was the navy, and to understand that was to know Dad's heart.

In the weeks after we buried Dad, Mom received a letter, postmarked Killeen, Texas. It wasn't from Jim, but from a stranger, a man named Bill Smith.

> Dear Mrs. Schuler,
>
> I am a friend of your son, Jim. I'm writing to tell you how very sorry I am about the death of your husband. Jim always

spoke so highly of him, and I wanted you to know you are all in my prayers during this difficult time. Jim is well and doing fine.

Best wishes,

Bill Smith

Naturally, this set our wheels spinning. Who was Bill Smith? Why was he writing to us when Jim was silent? It was a mystery. But soon after, a big sympathy card arrived from Jim. He wrote:

I wish I could be there with you. I love you, Mom.

One day the phone rang in my New York apartment. The voice on the other end of the line was not familiar to me—it was heavy, Southern-sounding. "How's it goin'?" he said.

A pause. "Who is this?" I finally asked.

"Don't you even know your own brother?" Now the voice was edgy, challenging. Jim.

"Oh," I tried to recover. "I didn't recognize you. I guess it's that Southern accent you've picked up." I laughed into the silence. I couldn't think of anything else to say, so then I said the wrong thing. "How did you get my number?"

"I see I'm bothering you," he said, offended.

"No . . . no . . ."

"Forget it," he said. "Take care."

And he was gone.

I had failed him again. What was wrong with me? Would it have killed me to give my brother a hearty welcome—to express delight at hearing from him? Over the years, I had convinced myself that the problems between us were all of Jim's making, but honestly, I had hardened my heart against him. As much as I complained that Jim could not get past who I was as a teenager, I, too, could not get past who Jim had become as an adult.

I waited for him to call back, thinking I'd try to do better the next time, but he didn't call again. The threads connecting us to Jim's life were popping one by one. The communications dwindled. Each letter was a carbon copy of the last:

I'm doing fine . . . I'm working . . . I'm playing golf . . . I promise to visit soon . . . I'm going to let you go now.

Sometimes we talked about launching Project Jim. We'd travel in a group, his siblings, riding into Texas like the cavalry, find him and bring him home. I like to think we really meant it. But like all vaguely uttered good intentions, this one simply got away from us.

Mom received a letter from Jim on August 14, 2001, two weeks after his fifty-third birthday:

Dear Mom,

I apologize for not writing for awhile, but things just seem to happen and it seems like time passes by so fast that before you know it another year has passed by.

I received the birthday card and pictures you sent, and Mom, you look great!

Everything here is fine, I'm feeling great. I had a physical last week and everything was fine.

I'm still working, but I think my job might be in jeopardy. Everyone is cutting back. We'll just have to wait and see. If it does happen, that will be all right. It will give me a chance to play more golf!

Mom, I hope the family is fine. I really do miss everyone. It will really be nice to see everyone when I come up, soon I hope.

Listen, Mom, I'm going to let you go. I hope this letter finds you well and happy. I will talk to you soon. Give everyone my love.

All my love,

Jim

The next day, Mom got the call. Jim was dead.

EIGHT

DO YOU REMEMBER ME?

HELLO OUT THERE. Here's a picture of me—the good lookin' one with the beer—and some buddies. It was taken just before the Tet Offensive. We was somewhere around Da Nang. Does anyone recognize me? Did anyone know me when I was in 'Nam? Does anyone remember me?

Cries for help by the thousands float in cyberspace, mostly unanswered. Their purpose isn't solely a hoped-for reunion, but a desperate, and often fruitless, effort to find others who can help them prove to the VA when and where they served, and what they experienced.

Is there anyone out there who served with——from April 15, 1966, to July 30, 1966? I've been told to secure names of persons who served with him during this time and at these locations to possibly secure proof of being in Vietnam during this time. He has prostate cancer and the VA is denying his claim of being in Vietnam. We've been told that "buddy" statements won't authenticate the service in Vietnam so am looking for a source more positive. Anyone?????

My husband was recently diagnosed with adenocarcinoma of the prostate. The VA wants us to jump through hoops to provide them with information they already have due to earlier disability claims. Now we start over again. We need to provide statements from other servicemen who served in Vietnam with —— to verify he was exposed to Agent Orange and in what areas he was exposed. We are on the AO register and have been for years but that doesn't seem to make any difference. If you know anyone who served with my husband in Vietnam we would appreciate any information you can provide.

Did you serve at Pleiku AFB 10/68 to 10/69? We received rocket fire daily, but the VA won't accept a claim for PTSD without a witness; rank, service number, and dates who can verify we were in a "combative situation." Can you help?

I am a Vietnam veteran looking for anyone who served in Duc Hoa from Oct. 70 to Oct. 71. I have liver cancer and have been denied VA benefits several times because I cannot provide evidence of my combat trauma. I need someone to help me with a written statement that they were in the same unit and place during these years. Your help will be greatly appreciated. God Bless You.

I originally thought I had gone through the war unscathed, but that is not so. So many died while I lived; many who went where I was to go but couldn't. I thought I had buried those thoughts so deep they would never come out again, but after thirty some odd years they busted out—in dreams I cannot remember, in super alertness. I sleep with knives. I am always looking for something to happen. I cry a lot if I see a combat movie. I cannot even remember my buddies from Nam's names. I am filing a claim for PTSD, but cannot remember names, times, or where. If any of you remember me or can help, I would appreciate it.

Sending calls for help into cyberspace is like spitting in the ocean. These veterans have little hope of actually connecting with one of their old unit members. More often than not, they aren't even sure whom they're hoping to find. Their messages are full of uncertainty and fragmented recollections, what they refer to as the CRS (*can't remember shit*) syndrome :

My memories aren't so good anymore . . . I've lost all the names.

I'm looking for a guy, I think his name was Jackie, we called him Slim, and he was from the South. Can't remember his last name.

One of the most poignant messages I came across simply read:

I'm looking for me. Does anyone remember where I was in Nam?

Before the Internet, these seekers would have had virtually no chance of finding their lost comrades. The Internet offers a tiny window of opportunity, but only if their old buddies are also looking for them. The process reminds me of the odd and hopeless personal ads I used to read on the back page of the *Village Voice*: "Our eyes met on the F train, January 2. You had dark hair and were wearing a blue coat. I felt a connection. Please respond to this ad if you felt it, too." Those ads held a certain fascination, a pathos—people reaching out in the darkness to locate a single unknown soul in a city of millions, spending their dollars on a hope and a prayer. I found a similarly raw plunge into the abyss here, but it was more desperate, because these sick and anguished veterans really *need* to find their buddies.

The proof-of-service runaround is a sad commentary on the VA's bureaucratic mentality. Most Americans have no idea that it goes on. To the average person, proof of service may seem like a given—doesn't the military keep records of those who served? Yes and no. The military may have your records (except when they get lost, as occurred in the unfortunate 1973 fire in St. Louis, which destroyed between sixteen and eighteen million records), but the details are slim. For example, my brother's military record shows the following information for his first year of service in Vietnam:

66-11-21 CO C 1ST ENGR BN 1ST INF DIV USARPAC

To decipher: He shipped to Vietnam on November 21, 1966, and was assigned to Company C, the First Engineer Battalion, attached to the First Infantry Division, under the umbrella of the U.S. Army Pacific Command. As the saying goes, that's all she wrote. There is no record of where he was, what he did, or what he encountered there. An entire year accounted for with this meager script. If Jim had ever tried to file a claim for PTSD, Agent Orange exposure, or any other service-related disability for that period, he would have been hard-pressed to come up with the requisite evidence.

What isn't recorded, unless you earned a Purple Heart, a Silver Star, or other citation that was specific to time and place, is the story of your service. You *say* you were in a firefight on such-and-such a date that caused traumatic brain injury. You *say* you witnessed your best buddies being blown apart by enemy fire and have post-traumatic stress disorder. You *say* you were in an area where Agent Orange was dumped by the ton and your cancer is a result.

OK, soldier. Prove it. And good luck.

Thirty or forty years after the fact, Vietnam veterans are still immersed in bureaucratic tangles over proof of service issues. Often their only hope is to collect buddy statements—affidavits from those with whom they served. But here's the real kick in the teeth. Buddy statements alone are not considered sufficient evidence to verify a claim unless they were written on official unit stationery and dated at the time of the actual event. It would be comic if it weren't so insanely tragic. Imagine being in the thick of battle when the wounded stop fighting for their lives and instead begin a furious search for stationery. It shocks the conscience.

Stories like the one told by Ram Chavez demonstrate how confusion can reign on the battlefield. Chavez—or "Doc," as he was known to his comrades—was the senior medic with the 199th Light Infantry Brigade ("Redcatchers") in 1967 and 1968, shortly before my brother joined the attached 87th Engineer Battalion. On May 1, 1968, his replacement, Harvey Lynn Cooley, arrived, and on May 5, Doc was scheduled to hop on a chopper back to base camp for his trip home. But he decided to stay an extra day to help the battalion surgeon set up an aid station at the next fire base. On May 6, one of the bodies that arrived at the aid station was Cooley, Doc's replacement; he had been killed on his second day in Vietnam. Doc made a decision to stay and replace his replacement, and was given permission to return to his original unit. On May 7, they received heavy enemy fire. Under ordinary circumstances, Doc would have received a Silver Star for his valor in action on that day.

The problem, according to army records, was that he wasn't there. "On paper, I had completed my tour in the field and was back at base camp," he said. "But I was there in the flesh."

It took Doc forty years, the aid of his congressman, and the supporting documentation of his former commanding officer, to prove to the army that he was in combat. He received his Silver Star in April 2008. Presumably, during those forty years, Doc dealt with many bureaucrats who simply decided he was lying. The tyranny of records prevailed over the simple truth of his bravery.

As veterans like Doc struggle mightily to find the evidence of their physical presence in places their minds can never forget, the Veterans Disability Benefits Claims Modernization Act of 2008 continues its snail's pace crawl through Congress. Having passed the House unanimously on July 30, 2008, it is now bogged down in the Senate.

The legislation, introduced by New York Democrat John Hall, is designed to overhaul a system that clearly isn't working. Among other improvements, Hall's legislation would make it easier for veterans who have served in combat zones to obtain benefits for post-traumatic stress disorder by removing the VA's requirement that they prove exposure to a specific "stressor."

"Veterans returning from war shouldn't have to leap hurdles to prove they experienced combat," said Hall, who serves as chairman of the House Veterans' Affairs Subcommittee on Disability Assistance and Memorial Affairs. "I've been to Iraq to meet with soldiers there, and I've talked to returning vets. There are no front lines, there is no rear. The risk of combat is clear and immediate, whether you're in Sadr City or the Green Zone."

And what if your combat injury is an enveloping sickness, not a specific injury? What if X doesn't mark the spot of your wound? It's not just PTSD that frustrates the veterans who file claims. The effects of Agent Orange have plagued countless Vietnam veterans who continue to struggle against almost impossible barriers to get their cases heard.

Soon after the end of the Vietnam War, many veterans who thought they'd dodged every bullet and returned home whole, began to suffer from a variety of strange symptoms, including bizarre tumors, and had children with birth defects. A pattern emerged, connecting their disabilities with exposure to a rainbow of herbicides used to destroy fields, rice paddies, and jungles in Vietnam. The most common was Agent Orange; there were also agents blue, pink, purple, and green. Contrary to popular belief, Agent Orange wasn't really orange; it was named for the orange bands around the barrels in which it was shipped. However, I have sometimes heard veterans recall quite vividly the heavy orange mist that hung in the air after spraying. I chalk it up to the power of sense memory, and the vision of sunlight on spray that might have given it an orange glow.

Early claims of damage from herbicide exposure were summarily dismissed until a group of veterans held a hunger strike in Washington during the Reagan administration. Congress was compelled to act, launching an Agent Orange study, but it was short-lived. Shoddy record keeping on the part of the military that fails to show exactly where Agent Orange was sprayed and which units were in the area at the time made it impossible to get an accurate picture.

In the following decades, more studies followed (three are still active today). The VA gradually came to accept that Agent Orange was a legitimate problem for hundreds of thousands of veterans. Today, the VA Web site contains much information that might help those who were exposed to file claims, and even includes a poster:

VA CARES

ABOUT VIETNAM VETERANS

AND OTHER VETERANS

EXPOSED TO

AGENT ORANGE

However, for those actually filing claims related to Agent Orange exposure, the bar is incredibly high. As Bishop Fulton J. Sheen once said, "The big print giveth, and the fine print taketh away." When veterans grow older, it is more difficult to prove that illnesses like prostate cancer or diabetes, which afflict the general aging population in higher numbers, can be linked to Agent Orange. The task of proving exposure is also very difficult, even though the military's own studies suggest that two million or more soldiers were stationed in areas where Agent Orange was used. If you were not "on the ground"—if, for example, you were stationed on a ship in the area—it is almost impossible to get a hearing.

A woman named Jennie Le Favre became something of a heroine to veterans struggling to get their AO claims heard. Jennie's husband, Jerry, served with the air force in Vietnam in 1968 and 1969. He was an airborne radio operator on C-130 aircraft that transported Agent Orange a couple of times a month. Jerry helped load and unload the containers with his bare hands, and he wrote to Jennie that skin was peeling off his hands in layers and he didn't know why. He said the doctor diagnosed "jungle rot," and he joked, "Are you still interested in me now that I'm a rotting old man of thirty-five?"

Jerry's radio position was in the cargo section of the aircraft, and it flew at low levels through mists of Agent Orange, with the cargo doors wide open and the mist drifting inside.

At the time, Jerry didn't think about the danger—few of the men did. He didn't know that the mist would be his death sentence long after he had put down the weapons of war. In May 1989, fifteen years after his retirement from the air force, Jerry was diagnosed with inoperable cancer of the lungs, liver, stomach, pancreas, lymph nodes, bone, and diaphragm. Jerry was also diagnosed with chronic obstructive pulmonary disease, degenerative joint disease, obstructive jaundice, anemia, cardiopulmonary arrest, congestive heart failure, and emphysema.

He died that December at the age of fifty-six. The death certificate listed the cause as "natural," which might have made Jennie laugh—she had a great sense of humor—if it weren't so darn tragic.

Jennie began a fourteen-year battle with the VA to have Jerry's death declared related to Agent Orange exposure. Her claims were rejected time and again. "In Vietnam, Jerry's nickname was Lucky Pierre," she wrote. "Jerry served in both the Korean and Vietnam wars, and he thought he had survived both wars. But he did not survive Vietnam, he was not so lucky after all. This is the treatment he receives for serving his country proudly for twenty-three years. This is the treatment his widow receives as well."

Along the way Jennie discovered many, many others who were facing the same problems. She started the Agent Orange Quilt of Tears, a support network for victims and their widows. The tapestries inspired by Jennie form a living wall, a traveling memorial of quilts featuring patches in honor of those who are sick or who have died due to AO exposure.

As Jennie built a community of support, she continued to launch appeals with the VA to posthumously have Jerry declared an Agent Orange victim. "When am I going to stop?" she asked. "Never! I'll never quit, as long as I can help people heal." Regrettably, Jennie lost her own fight; she died in 2004. But the Quilt of Tears has been picked up by others, and it lives on.

Possibly the loneliest veterans in the world are Gulf War veterans who suffer grave disabilities from what is called Gulf War syndrome. The Gulf War was a mere blip on our screens, over and done with before we knew it. With relatively few military casualties, the Gulf War is considered a great success. But about a year after the end of the war, some veterans started displaying mysterious symptoms—rashes, chronic pain, fatigue, unusual cancers, and digestive ailments. At first, there was a lot of scoffing about their symptoms. The familiar old denial machine went into action, trying to paint the soldiers as slackers, whiners, and frauds.

The very nature of Gulf War syndrome made it difficult to diagnose. The symptoms were varied and inconclusive, and there was no obvious single source. Complicating the issue, many of those claiming to have symptoms had not even been in the Gulf during the war; they had been at U.S. bases on standby alert. How could their symptoms be explained?

One answer, according to many experts who have studied Gulf War syndrome, may be the experimental drugs that service people were required to take—drugs that were believed to provide resistance to chemical weapons exposure. At the time, there was a near panic about the likelihood that Saddam Hussein would use chemical weapons against our troops. While there was never a direct hit, some soldiers in the Gulf were peripherally exposed to chemical agents such as Sarin.

Today, about 30 percent of the 700,000 men and women who served during the first Persian Gulf War have registered in the Gulf War Illness database set up by the American Legion. Some still suffer a baffling array of serious medical problems that have left them ill for many years. They, too, are engaged in the search for proof:

> I am suffering horribly and am looking for buddy statement from someone that might have been there with me suffering through Khamisiya, the DU from the tanks. I was exposed to Sarin big time the whole company went down. Anyone out the in theater near 3/8 cav let me know. I'm stuck at 50% and need buddy statements!!! Call me if you think you can help.

I have been fighting with my VA doctors trying to get help with GWS. I have been to 4 different clinics. None of the neurologists that the VA has shoved me off on have a clue as to how to treat or recognize my problems. My biggest concern is my headaches. They have become so disabling that I can't even hold down a job on a regular basis. Unfortunately for me the only thing that helps me to function as a relatively normal human being is medication, none of which any neurologist that I've seen is willing to prescribe. I don't sleep at night. The sleep medication that they gave me for awhile caused me to begin to sleep walk.

I spent 10 hours (one-way) on a Greyhound bus getting to my new doctor's appointment yesterday to find out that they won't help me, and that they claim there is no test available to them to detect GWS. One doctor in one of the many VA clinics said that I was given a contaminated Anthrax vaccination while in the service. Now this doctor was promoted and no longer sees patients. No other doctor that I've been passed off to seems to have any clue as to how to treat me.

Now they want to take me off of all my medications claiming that the only reason why I have a headache, among the list of other ailments (memory loss, fatigue, muscle and joint pain, sleeping disorders, fibromyalgia, blood in my urine), is the medication.

Is there anyone out there that can point me in the right direction of a doctor within the system who knows what they are doing? Is there anyone out there that can help me. I'm nearing financial ruin over all of this, and I don't think my wife could stand me to pee in the bathtub again from the sleep walking. I've put her through a lot.

The process of filing a claim usually begins with a phone call to one of the VA's fifty-seven regional offices. Anyone who has ever spoken with veterans about their experiences with VA help lines has heard the stories of frustration with these phone calls.

In 2002 and again in 2004, concerned about the number of complaints about its call centers, the VA executed a Mystery Caller Telephone Service Quality Assessment Program to evaluate the quality of information and support veterans were receiving from help lines.

The "mystery callers" were investigators with the VA who placed 1,089 calls to VA centers, posing as friends and relatives of veterans asking about possible benefits. Many of these calls, detailed in reports released via the Freedom of Information Act, showed a troubling lack of responsiveness. According to a VA internal memo, in 2004, 22 percent of responses were "completely incorrect," 23 percent were "minimally correct," and 20 percent were "partially correct." Only 19 percent were "completely correct," and 16 percent "mostly correct." And the VA's report concluded that veterans were not only being given the wrong advice, they were also frequently treated with rudeness and contempt by the operators. Here's an example:

MYSTERY CALLER: My father served in Vietnam in 1961 and 1962. Is there a way he can find out if he was exposed to Agent Orange?
VA SERVICE REPRESENTATIVE: He should know if they were spreading that chemical out there. He would be the only one to know. OK. (Hangs up laughing).

While the VA offered assurances that it was taking steps to improve training and procedures for telephone operators, a 2006 congressional inquiry showed there was still a long way to go.

VA officials and union representatives revealed some obvious contradictions in procedures. For example, although there were daily performance standards requiring that each representative answer sixty-four calls, the VA denied that there was any time limit imposed on calls. Figure it out: If your performance is measured on the volume of calls you handle, what's the incentive for taking the time to give callers a careful hearing?

Journalist Martin Schram, who first made the mystery caller scandal public and wrote about it in his excellent book, *Vets Under Siege*, has called for a total revamping of the VA rules and procedures that would make it easier for help-desk representatives to understand and explain them. "And in the process," Schram writes, "perhaps it is not naïvely utopian to suggest that the new and improved VA rules and procedures be made so straight-forward that they could actually be understood by the customers the VA is in business to serve—America's military veterans."

As much as one wants to believe that veteran support is genuine and made in good faith—the "thanks of a grateful nation"—there are just too many examples of this not being true. I'm not interested in beating up the VA. Overall, the department tries hard to perform an insurmountable task, often without the proper funds. The VA's mission, set out by Abraham Lincoln—"to care for him who shall have borne the battle and for his widow and his orphan"—is, for the most part, sincerely pursued. But the VA's efforts must be backed by a national will, and reflected in the budget if there is to be any hope of meeting the demand. Already overwhelmed, the agency expects the number of new vets entering the system from Iraq and Afghanistan to reach 600,000. And that's a conservative estimate.

Meanwhile, the VA scrambles to find the money any way it can. Unfortunately, that might mean sacrificing one group of deserving veterans for another. In 2005, David Chu, the under-secretary of defense for personnel and readiness, told Congress, "Benefits that apply mainly to retirees and their families are making it harder for the Pentagon to afford financial incentives for today's military." He argued, "Congress has gone too far in expanding military retiree benefits. They are starting to crowd out two things: First, our ability to reward the person who is bearing the burden right now in Iraq or Afghanistan. Second, they are undercutting our ability to finance the new gear that is going to make that military person successful five, ten, fifteen years from now."

Not surprisingly, veterans were outraged. Retired Army Colonel Harry Riley blasted back, "Mr. Chu, without rational justification, makes broad and sweeping statements identifying military retiree benefits as the enemy of our active force. I wonder if Mr. Chu ever considered how 'hard' it was at Normandy, in the jungles of the South Pacific, or the freezing battlefields of Korea as he sits in his office and denigrates these old warriors seeking benefits they earned."

Robbing Peter (older veterans) to pay Paul (active military and more recent veterans of the Afghanistan and Iraq wars) is a lousy policy by any measure. It is this kind of attitude that leaves veterans feeling that they have few friends in Washington.

However, many veterans groups see a reason for optimism in Barack Obama's selection of former general Eric Shinseki to head the Department of Veterans Affairs. Shinseki's history of service (including a battlefield injury in Vietnam that took off part of a foot) is impressive, and he is known to be an unflinching advocate for the troops. During the Bush administration, Shinseki risked his career when he challenged Defense Secretary Donald Rumsfeld's Iraq troop plan. Shinseki told the Senate Armed Services Committee that success in Iraq would require far more forces than Rumsfeld claimed. Shinseki's outspokenness was seen as a career-ending move, and he was forced to retire from the army within weeks of his testimony. His return to public service, in this important advocacy role, is seen not only as a personal victory, but a sign that the stumbling bureaucracy of the VA may be in for a long needed overhaul.

Paul Rieckhoff is a powerful man—six foot two and 240 pounds. His muscular frame strains inside his neat business suit, and he cuts an imposing figure with his bald head and strong face, resembling a modern day Jesse Ventura. He looks much older than his thirty-three years, but his voice is soft, his words measured. Rieckhoff has become a familiar face on cable talk shows, where he speaks with nonpartisan passion about supporting veterans. He is a voice of quiet reason and strength in a medium where the rhetoric is often turned to the highest decibel level. He represents a new generation of veterans, and, I predict, a new generation of leaders. We'll be seeing Paul Rieckhoff for a long time.

Rieckhoff joined the army reserves in 1999, after graduating from Amherst College with a degree in political science. He was sent to Iraq in 2003, and, as he writes in *Chasing Ghosts*, his book about his war experience, he was an ambivalent warrior. The opening line of the book, "George Bush had better be fucking right," were the words he scrawled in his journal as he headed for Iraq.

Back home and out of the army, Rieckhoff became one of the first veterans to challenge the war. Disillusioned by the lack of support for veterans, in 2004, he established the Iraq and Afghanistan Veterans of America (IAVA). Finding the American people to be largely disassociated from the war and its consequences, Rieckhoff wanted to shed light on the reality—to shake the public from its stupor. It offended him that while soldiers were dying in Iraq, the American public was out shopping or obsessing about who would win *American Idol*.

What is most notable about Paul Rieckhoff is his determination to measure support by practical actions. He is not a man who says, "This is how we must *feel*." Instead, he says, "This is what we must *do*." He has crafted ten steps the Obama administration should take to ensure veteran support. His formula cuts straight to the heart of the matter, and is a strikingly intelligent and comprehensive list:

1. Ensure thorough, professional, and confidential mental health screening: Mandatory and confidential mental health and traumatic brain injury screening by a mental health professional for all troops, both before and at least ninety days after a combat tour.

2. Advance-fund VA health care: To avoid a break in care when VA budgets are passed late (a frequent occurrence), ensure timely funding of veterans' health-care programs one year in advance.

3. Overhaul the military and veterans' disability system: A complete overhaul is needed in order to streamline the process and provide adequate benefits to our wounded troops.

4. Cut the claims backlog in half: The claims backlog, numbering in the hundreds of thousands, must be cut in half within the new president's first year in office.

5. End the passive VA system: Although the VA offers a wide array of benefits and services, many veterans do not know what they are eligible for. The VA must more aggressively advertise their services, especially online and in rural areas.

6. Combat the shortage of mental health professionals:
The VA must be authorized to bolster its mental
health workforce with adequate psychiatrists,
psychologists, and social workers to meet the
demands of returning Iraq and Afghanistan veterans.

7. Create tax incentives for patriotic employers: Give
tax credits for hiring veterans, including National
Guardsmen and reservists, and those at risk for
homelessness. Also give tax credits for employers
when reservist employees are called for duty,
comparable to the difference between the service
member's civilian salary and military pay.

8. Fight homelessness among veterans: 50,000 new
vouchers should be issued to house homeless
veterans, and the next president should end
homelessness among veterans by the end of his
first term.

9. Give families access to mental health support:
Military families should have improved access to
mental health services, and active-duty families
should be given unlimited access to mental health
care, including family and marital counseling on
military bases.

10. Repeal the waiver of high-deployment pay: The
high deployment allowance should be enforced, and
should include service members who are currently
in a combat theatre and have served more than
365 days in a hazardous duty zone over the past
two years (for active-duty troops) or over the past
five years (for those in the reserve component).

Rieckhoff's ten-point plan underscores how scattershot most VA, Pentagon, and congressional approaches to veteran services have been in recent decades. They rush to put out brush fires, respond to occasional public outcries, and frequently politicize their positions. But the VA lacks a long-term mission that places priorities in context. The public, and especially the veteran population, rarely has a sense that the VA is heading anywhere, except deeper into a morass of unfulfilled promises.

In the end, it is up to us. Public will is the cornerstone of action, and the sad truth is that except for the occasional sparks of media attention, to be a veteran today is to be invisible, especially if you are disabled or suffer mental health problems. We don't like to be reminded of the costs of war, or to have the thrill of military victory dampened by evidence of its scars.

When soldiers returning from Vietnam were met by angry protesters screaming "Baby killers!" and a nonexistent military support system, they were devastated. Discharged into a land that refused to acknowledge them, they became a lost generation of soldiers. Later, the public indifference to their needs became something of a scandal, and we promised, "Never again."

Yet here we are—yes, *again*. As thousands of veterans raise the tormented cry, "Does anyone remember me?" the response is weak and erratic—heavy static on a lifeline.

NINE

FINDING JIM

2004

GRAINY, SMUDGED photocopies provided the first concrete information of my brother's twenty years with the U.S. Army. I squinted trying to read them. I tried a magnifying glass, and then attempted to enlarge them on my printer. What a small, sorry pile of papers to represent a career of service. Jim's records contained a bare minimum of information. As for so many others, my brother's life had been reduced to a series of numbers and letters, the frustrating shorthand of the military. Jim had been but one numerical cog in a wheel that turns and turns and turns.

My eyes strained to read the fine print. My head ached from the effort.

Three years after his death, I had decided to embark on a mission to find my brother, but it was slow going. I had hoped that Jim's military records would begin to flesh out his life. There were so many unanswered questions, so many empty parts, so many years unaccounted for. Could his service records open a window into his life outside of the service?

Absent in Jim's records was the flesh-and-blood reality of his career—the day-to-day doings; the actions, events, and relationships of a life spent in the military.

I imagined there were many others like me, receiving the same large manila envelope in the mail, eagerly tearing it open, scouring the pages, looking for the words that would begin to fill in some of the missing details of a loved one's service, provide color to an inadequate sketch. At first, there's optimism: there are so many pages! But soon the optimism turns to disappointment. The sparse, fill-in-the-blanks nature of the documents is woefully unsatisfactory.

For the novice, it is daunting. Trying to puzzle out the forms, I sometimes had to laugh, bewildered. The military has forever marched forward on a series of numbers and codes. And once I sorted out the basics provided to me, it was demoralizing how little information there was, and how contradictory some of it seemed.

I was struck anew with sympathy for the veterans who were mired in the frustrating process of trying to prove aspects of their service in order to gain essential benefits. If the army, with its vast bureaucracy, could not supply answers, how could one lone person?

Since the day he died, I knew I wanted to write about my brother. The idea became even stronger as I watched another generation of young soldiers ship off to war. I wanted to fill in the blank years that led up to Jim's death, and somehow bring him home. Impossible though it was, I wanted to return Jim whole to our family. But I also had a greater purpose.

My brother's story was not unique. Countless other families have faced similar confusion and heartbreak. By shining a light on Jim's life, maybe I could help illuminate a path for them.

Once I committed myself to the task of learning about Jim, I realized that it would be an uphill battle. The chief enemy was time—the way that years corrode a life's experiences and relationships, turning them all to ashes and dust as surely as the earth does to a body in the grave.

Searching for family secrets is like excavating an ancient archeological sight: carefully examining and cleaning off each tiny fragment, setting it aside for further investigation, sometimes plumbing deep caverns that yield nothing at all. It was tedious and frustrating work.

Where were the connections, the people who would show me the way? Where was the unbreakable storyline that would allow me to say, "This was my brother. This was his life"? The barriers to truth seemed at times insurmountable.

My initial task was to resurrect the details of Jim's service—first, by ordering his records, and second, by trying to find people who might have served with him—who knew him during the war, or in its aftermath.

There were many enlistment and reenlistment forms in Jim's files; he "re-upped" five times. In his initial enlistment papers, dated 1966, I found the familiar young Jim: red hair, blue eyes, five foot ten, 147 pounds, O-positive blood. He was still a boy then, with a boy's height and weight. He hadn't yet finished growing. By his fifth and last reenlistment in 1980, he had grown to six feet and weighed 172 pounds.

On each form was Jim's signature. It's funny how you can recognize a signature after forty years. In the course of my search, I heard from a Vietnamese woman who thought she'd known Jim. She didn't have a photo, but she had a note with a signature, which she sent me. I knew with complete certainty that it was not Jim by the handwriting.

In twenty years, Jim had lived and served in thirteen different locations. They were, in order: Fort Ord, California; Fort Leonard Wood, Missouri; Lai Khe, Vietnam; Fort Carson, Colorado; Fort Lawton, Washington; Long Binh, Vietnam; Fort Lewis, Washington; Vilseck, Germany; Dalat, Vietnam; Fort Rucker, Alabama; Fort Campbell, Kentucky; Berlin, Germany; and Fort Hood, Texas.

He had many assignments. Jim was a combat engineer, a combat demolition specialist, a combat construction specialist, a dump-truck driver, a soil analyst, an MP, a platoon sergeant, a recon sergeant, and a squad leader.

There was a stack of certificates in his files showing various awards, letters of commendation, and special training. There was documentation for his Purple Heart, with a bit of new information about his injuries. I'd known that Jim received the Purple Heart in December 1968. That, at least, was clear from the medal we recovered, and from a certificate in his records. But his file listed two separate incidents when he was wounded:

- Frag wound to right side of face (68/12/09) / bullet
- Wound to left leg (69/03/08)

My mind flashed back to Jim pulling up his pant leg on that afternoon in Seattle, showing me the scar. I'd always assumed that it was the wound for which he'd received his Purple Heart. I never knew about the bullet fragments to the face—the injury in battle that earned him the medal. There was no scar from that wound. Less than three months after the frag wound to his face, he'd received the wound to his left leg. Apparently, it wasn't in combat, so he wasn't awarded a second Purple Heart. It might have been a construction accident. I had heard about many of them, some fatal, as the engineers plowed through the rough jungle astride their massive plows.

Like many Americans, I have become educated during the current wars about the frequency of "noncombat" injuries, which take a toll that is every bit as great as enemy fire. Men and women can be crippled for life and even killed during these incidents. It seems callous to me that their injuries don't receive the acknowledgment of valor that they deserve. From my point of view, if you're serving in a combat zone, you're in combat.

It would have been nice to know more about the circumstances of Jim's injuries, but the records gave no details. I will forever wonder if, boxed away somewhere in a warehouse, there are field reports that describe those incidents. Maybe, maybe not. It seems that the fog of war never lifts.

One document in Jim's records caught my eye. It was a GED certificate, dated 1977. Jim had been in the army for ten years by the time he finally received a high-school equivalency diploma. That bothered me. He had invested in the army, body and soul, cutting short his high-school education to serve in Vietnam. He had reenlisted twice by 1977, but the army had not seen fit to make sure he earned his high-school diploma. Jim had hopes of career advancement, so it was vital that he have some sort of an education. At least that's the way I saw it. Knowing Jim's high expectations, his plan to advance up the ranks, it was clearly an impossible dream. Everyone understands that education matters, especially if one expects to become an officer. Sadly, in this arena Jim didn't seem to have had a mentor.

And yet, by 1980, Jim's career had taken an upward turn that clearly indicated he was being prepared to take on greater responsibilities. He'd gone through Air Assault School with the 101st Airborne Division that year, and had also been sent to and graduated from the elite Jungle Warfare School in Panama. He'd reached his highest ranking (E-7), and was a platoon sergeant. He'd been assigned to the Berlin Brigade, which everyone agreed was a plum posting.

Then something happened to Jim.

It was right there in his file, a single page that shocked me out of my skin because of its ominous heading: "Record of Court Martial Conviction."

Like most people, I know of courts-martial mainly from movies and books. They are always portrayed as dramatic, career-ending events, followed by years in a military prison. But it turns out that there are many different types of courts-martial. Jim's was a "special" court-martial, under Article 134, which, while serious, was comparable to a misdemeanor.

Article 134 is a catchall category encompassing offenses that are not specifically listed in the manual for courts-martial—that is to say, "all disorders and neglects to the prejudice of good order and discipline in the armed forces, all conduct of a nature to bring discredit upon the armed forces, and crimes and offenses not capital, of which persons subject to this chapter may be guilty." Article 134 is sometimes sarcastically referred to as "write your own law" or "court-martial for being stupid."

During his final year in Berlin, it seems that Jim ended up owing some German civilians a fair sum of money for that time—$5,900 to be exact. It might have been a gambling debt or an unpaid car loan. It could have been anything. But it was serious enough to warrant the attention of his superiors, and serious enough to convene a court-martial. Jim was found guilty according to Article 134, and fined a reduction in grade to E-6. A reprimand was placed in his permanent file. The reduction in grade was serious business. Not only did it affect his ability to be promoted, but it also meant a substantial decrease in pay.

But it was the date of Jim's court-martial that held the most significance for me. It glared at me from the page, explaining everything that had happened during his last visit home.

It happened in May 1984. Jim had faced the court-martial one month before that fateful trip. "Oh, shit," I muttered, picturing Jim's face during that visit, remembering how I thought something was wrong the moment I saw him. And now, here it was—the answer. If we had only known. It explained so much. Too proud, too ashamed to reveal this blot on his record and his career, Jim had, instead, acted out his disappointment and fury. He obviously felt that our family would have been unable to handle the news without delivering a harsh judgment. He may have been right. He probably imagined that we'd all been waiting for him to screw up, and now he had.

If he had quietly taken Dad and Mom aside and told them what had happened, I believe they would have appreciated his honesty. They would have tried to help him. And, most significantly, they would have been more alert to his moods during that wedding weekend, and maybe things would have ended differently. But there's no point in speculating, because none of that happened. Jim felt he couldn't trust his family with the truth. It was a devastating blow to his image as an elite professional soldier. And it may have killed his career.

When I thought that I had gathered enough information, I began the long, slow march through the Internet veteran Web sites and military unit pages, looking for someone who might have known my brother. I cast a line into that bottomless sea, along with so many other vets and their families, praying for a nibble.

It was easy enough to find veterans who had served in the same battalions and the same companies as Jim. But even that was akin to opening the phone book in a town and assuming that a random individual would know another random individual. There are approximately nine hundred soldiers in a battalion, and over one hundred in a company. And given the nature of service in Vietnam, there was a lot of splitting off from the main companies, and a lot of comings and goings, as each person's length of tour began at a different point in time. Also, the people who join these Internet groups represent only a small percentage of the total number of vets who are out there, and many of them served in Vietnam during different periods than Jim.

Still, the Internet was a seductive lure. As unlikely as it seemed, I was drawn in by the idea that among all the veterans searching for wartime buddies, someone could be searching for Jim. It was a weird kind of popularity contest. I wanted to be able to whisper in my prayers, "Hey, Jim, your old buddies are still out there, looking for you."

I also studied hundreds of old snapshots taken during the Vietnam War and posted on the Web, certain I would find Jim's face in one of them. The photos pulled me in. I couldn't stop looking at them, and every once in a while I thought I saw Jim's face, appearing like a mirage, but I was always wrong. They all looked so much alike, those young engineers, stripped to the waist, sitting on plows, their young bodies gleaming in the scorching Southeast Asian sun. They posed in groups, clutching each other and grinning, their youth and bravado apparent, smiles broadened by camaraderie and the spirit of adventure.

I was aided in my search by some of the kindest men I have ever known. The brotherhood of veterans came together to help. These guys didn't know me, and most had never known Jim. But they put out the word, showed his picture around at reunions, and tried to help me in any way they could. Their motivation was pure; if a brother was lost, they would help find him. Their minds sifted through fragments of memory in an effort to summon Jim's face in their own worn mental scrapbooks. But as one veteran told me, "I know I served with your brother. I was right there during the same period. But I no longer remember any names, and even the faces all look the same to me. I'm so sorry."

In the end, I located two men who had served with Jim in Vietnam, and while they, too, had shaky memories, they did recall a few details. And even more valuable, they provided me with a sense of what their life as combat engineers had been like, and what they'd all been doing over there during the war.

"Jim and I were together in the pit," Bill G. told me. "He was a strong guy, and so was I. We'd spend twelve hours digging trenches, and it seemed like there were millions of red ants crawl-ing out of those holes." Bill was extremely compassionate about Jim's fate. "I was one of the lucky ones," he told me. "I've been married for forty years to the same woman. I have wonderful chil-dren and grandchildren. I'm retired now, and my life is good. But I never stop thinking about the guys who weren't so lucky. My thoughts and prayers are with your brother. Just know that he served honorably."

Christian B., another Vietnam buddy, remembered being in Lai Khe with Jim. "I was scared every minute I was in Vietnam," he said. "Jim never seemed scared. He always volunteered for the worst patrols. The Donut Dollies loved him."

Donut Dollies, I learned, were young women volunteers working with the Red Cross. They were recruited from college campuses and assigned to military bases, where they organized recreation programs for the troops. Jim first encountered Donut Dollies when he was at Long Binh. Theirs was, by all accounts, a difficult job—morale building in the worst place on earth. They are rarely acknowledged, a glaring oversight in my opinion.

Christian, who is active in veteran organizations, was not that surprised to hear about Jim's troubles. "We were just teenagers in Nam," he said. "How were we supposed to know how to feel? I had my own drinking problem for a while, but by the grace of God I came through OK. It hurts me to see so many that didn't."

I treasured the snippets of information I learned about Jim's service in Vietnam; I was glad to have anything at all. And I came to see that it didn't really matter if a particular veteran actually served with or remembered Jim. The veterans I spoke with *knew* him in the most important ways. They could feel for him as deeply as if he'd been their best buddy. They were all brothers.

If Jim were alive today, he would find a supportive, non-judgmental community among these men. They would care.

They would understand. My heart aches that he never had the opportunity to be embraced by this incredible group of kind souls, who would have offered him kinship and support.

The men I found experienced varying degrees of success at putting Vietnam behind them. They all talked about it. But even those who lived stable lives knew others like my brother who hadn't done so well. They formed a network of support that was truly impressive, reaching out to their comrades from across the nation after receiving a phone call or a note, attempting in their small ways to stand as a bulwark to the wounded. In their view, every soldier's life was meaningful and deserved respect.

More daunting than the details of Jim's military service was the task of recovering his lost years after retirement, and answering the questions that still disturbed us about his final days and the circumstances of his death. Jim died alone, in a shabby apartment in Killeen, Texas, two blocks from Fort Hood. His body wasn't discovered for three days, long after decay had set in. The coroner's report was cursory and maddeningly vague about the cause of death, stating only "heart failure." It wasn't much of an explanation. Had Jim been ill? We found no evidence that he had been receiving medical treatment. There were no bottles of medicine in his apartment. The women at Jim's building who interacted with him every day had not noticed that he was sick, and no friends came forward who could provide even the slightest clue. Nor was there evidence of foul play. We were afraid to speculate about whether or not Jim had committed suicide. The open questions strained our imaginations and cried out for answers.

What happened during all those years? What was he thinking? What was he feeling? What was he doing?

Here, I had one frail lead—Bill Smith. We had never found out anything about the man who wrote a sympathy card to our mother in 1996 after Dad died, and we hadn't heard from him again. The address on his card might have changed in the decade since his letter to Mom. But I sat down and wrote him a letter, hoping to open a door:

Dear Mr. Smith,

I would appreciate a moment of your time on a personal matter. Twelve years ago you knew my brother, Jim Schuler. I know this because of a lovely letter you wrote to my mother in Seattle, on Jim's behalf. (She still has it!) As you know, Jim died in 2001 in Killeen, Texas. As a family we have struggled greatly with remorse and regret over our alienation from Jim in his final years. The last time any of us saw him was in 1984. We knew he had problems, but he chose to make himself a mystery to us, only communicating in very brief terms. We don't know what his life was like. We don't even know how he died. The coroner said "natural causes," as if there is anything natural about a fifty-three-year-old man dying in his sleep.

The thing you have to know about our family is that we are very close knit. Jim was the second of nine children. I was born two years after him, and when we were kids we did everything together. We have surmised that Jim's Vietnam experience created wounds we couldn't see and were too stupid to know how to address. We know he had an alcohol problem for many years. We tried to tell him how proud we were of him and of his service, but he never believed it.

Our mother is elderly now, and every day she mourns her dead son and wishes she could have done more for him. Since you were his friend during a period in the 1990s, maybe you could fill in a couple of blanks. We're not looking for rosy scenarios—just the truth of who Jim was in the days he was lost to us.

I would be most grateful—we all would—if you could offer any information or insight. Would you be willing to speak to me?

Sincerely,

Catherine Whitney

Days after I sent the letter, I received a response.

Dear Catherine,

It was indeed a surprise to receive your letter concerning your brother Jim. I can understand and empathize with your family's need to know what happened to him, especially your mother's concern. I would be happy to talk to you about him.

Sincerely,

Bill Smith

I read Bill's letter through misty eyes. Yes, he knew Jim. Yes, they were friends. Yes, he would talk to me. Hallelujah!

Bill Smith is a warm, caring guy who had given a lot of thought to Jim's life and death. A few years older than my brother, he had also retired from the army at Fort Hood. He had been drafted in 1963 and served as a helicopter pilot, retiring as a major. He lived in a small town near Killeen, Texas. He and Jim had met in retirement and formed a bond as Vietnam veterans.

"Yes, Jim had an alcohol problem, as many veterans do," he told me. "It is a way to forget for a short period of time the things that happened in the past. All the time I knew Jim I never saw him drive a car. He always took a taxi wherever he went. I don't know if that was because of the drinking, or if he'd lost his license."

He admitted, "In a way, I am like Jim. I have been through three marriages, and now I'm alone. However, I made some major changes in my life—the main one being that I haven't had a drink for many years. I've tried to get on with the life I have left. Drinking was a major problem for me, and once I conquered that, I knew I'd be OK. Jim could never beat that problem, and in the end that's what probably got him. "

Bill confirmed that Jim had not been employed during the final years of his retirement, and his reference in letters to having a job was just one piece of the comforting fiction he had spun for the family. "Jim may have had a part-time job from time to time, but during the years I knew him he wasn't working and was living off of his retirement pay, which is not a lot. I would see him almost every day until the last week of each month, but not that week, because he probably ran out of money and was waiting for the check."

Bill recounted stories of Jim's alcohol-fueled anger. "He could become aggressive when he drank. Several times, I and the other guys had to hold him back from pounding someone who had said the wrong thing to him. That was Jim. But he could also be charming and gentle. In my opinion, Jim seemed to have low self-esteem. For some reason, he never felt he was as good as the rest of us. To this day I don't know why he felt that way. He was as good or better than any of us."

I asked Bill if he knew anything about how Jim had died. "Was he sick?"

He told me that Jim had been suffering from chest pains during his last year, and Bill had urged him to get medical treatment, or even a checkup, but he'd always refused. Did Jim feel invulnerable? Did he just not care? I never believed my brother was suicidal, at least not in the sense of taking bold action, but self-neglect is a form of slow suicide.

"Vietnam left many scars on all of us," Bill said. "They were not necessarily physical scars, but psychological scars. I still have them to this day. I know that Jim saw and did things over there that no one could ever understand. So did I. We all did. They never go away. They have a profound effect. After Vietnam, the service was not so good about providing help to people, and that's why so many veterans have suffered so much."

I confessed to Bill that I felt a lot of guilt over my lack of compassion and support during the darkest years of Jim's life. In this regard, Bill was wiser than I, and had a great spirit of forgiveness. "Guilt is a useless emotion," he said. "You have to let go of it. I know that's easier said than done. Hindsight is always better than foresight, and we all wish that we had done things differently. In the end, no matter what help and understanding that you may have given to Jim, he had to be the one to make the changes, and he was not willing or able to do that. I wish I had done more now, but that is in the past and there is nothing I can do about it. Maybe the lesson is that we have to do for others."

Bill also had an urgent message for our mother. "I don't think any of this was her fault," he said. "Please tell your mother that she had a great son. Tell her that he has friends here who still think of him."

I smiled, grateful. I knew my mother would appreciate hearing that.

Did I succeed? Did I find Jim? I wish I could say yes, but the verdict on my search isn't that simple. Jim took most of his secrets to the grave. But here, finally, is what I concluded about my brother's life. Here is the story I can tell about Jim, with love and mourning, and a newfound respect for all he contributed and all he suffered. It is, I know, the story of many men and women.

When I first contacted Bill Smith, I told him that I wasn't looking for rosy scenarios, just the truth. And the truth is a heavy weight. But I also didn't want my brother's life to seem like a caricature. I wanted to give him peace with dignity.

Jim was a boy when he went to war, but he brought some demons with him into combat. Some of those demons served him well. His aggressive temperament, his recklessness, his deep need to always come out on top of the pile may have ultimately ensured his survival. His positive attributes were also on display: his courage, his tireless work ethic, his abiding love of the army, his willingness to raise his hand time after time and say, "Send me!"

Although Jim was honorably discharged from the army, the court-martial in 1984 began a downward slide. Then, a later episode near the end of his service involving an alcohol-related car accident sealed his fate. The army was done with him. He could retire honorably with his lifer's pension. They thanked him for his twenty years, and let him know it was best to leave this way. In effect, his commanding officers said, "We're going to let you go now. You are dismissed."

He was only thirty-seven years old—in real-world time, a young man. He had experience, skills, and passion that might have been valuable to the army for another twenty years of service. He would have been proud to serve in the Gulf War. He would have been proud to serve in Iraq. Even as an older version of the outstanding professional soldier and combat engineer he had once been, Jim would have continued to raise his hand and say, "Send me," until the day he died. But wiser heads prevailed, and so he was retired.

Those same wise heads did not, however, try to throw him a lifeline while he was in their midst. In the 1980s, there was still little acknowledgment of the problem many soldiers had with alcohol. There were no treatment centers, no sense that someone with a drinking problem could be rehabilitated. That has changed dramatically in recent years, but back then, if you had a drug or alcohol problem that could no longer be hidden and controlled, you were out.

At first, Jim might have tried to adjust to civilian life, find a job, settle down, and make something of his new life. But according to his friends in Killeen, he never really worked again. From the time of his retirement until his death, he lived in the same rundown apartment, and no one knows what he did for hours on end, day after day, week after week, month after month, year after lonely year, inside his spartan monk's cell.

Shame and defeat are a bitter combination for an old warrior, and civilian life broke Jim. What could he do with his skills now? How could he thrive in a world full of civilians? Did he miss the routines of twenty years duration? You can bet that he did. The catalyzing fury and devotion on display during his army years, the toughness, the aggressive hostility, were soon replaced by despair and a sense of worthlessness. He did not reach out for love or much companionship, and those choices defined his final solitary days.

For Jim, the thanks of a grateful nation amounted to a pension of less than $800 a month after taxes. No one expected a thirty-seven-year-old to live off retirement pay. He was supposed to go out there and get a regular job, but clearly he was incapable of doing that. He was too proud to ask for help, and he distanced himself from his family so we wouldn't know how he was living, or see his destitution.

Alone in his barren apartment, estranged from his family, heartsick at the end, I imagine Jim's thoughts often strayed to the only time in his life when he truly felt alive. The army had made him believe he was somebody special. Maybe war gave him a purpose, but ultimately it was peace he craved.

—

TEN

WATCH
FIRES
BURNING

O N THE EVENING that precedes Memorial Day each year, my neighbors and I are drawn to the Piermont Pier like moths to a flame. We walk late at night along a long roadway lined with high cattails and marsh grasses that leads to the pier, a manmade strip of land, stretching out into the Hudson River from the old mill town of Piermont, New York. It is a magical setting of tidal marshes that serve as host to nature's bounty. Swans nest in the high grasses and reeds; ducks and geese come in droves to feed from the copious plant life. Because this part of the Hudson River is estuarial, there is a variety of fish and abundant crabs. It is a birding paradise, with kingfishers, great blue herons, mourning doves, blue jays, robins, goldfinch, sparrows, cardinals, and orioles, as well as the occasional peregrine falcon and red-tailed hawk floating on the winds, searching the shallows of the river for their next meal.

The Piermont Pier has a long history as a centerpiece of the industrial era that drove the growth of the entire region, but especially the mills of Piermont. It was initially constructed to serve as a freight train conduit, the railroad cars then loaded on barges for the trip down the river to Manhattan.

But the pier also enjoys a more recent history as a troop embarkation point, and it bears impressive military credentials. During World War II, more than 1.3 million servicemen were processed at nearby Camp Shanks in Orangetown before marching along the road leading to the end of the pier, boarding troop ships, and traveling down the river and out into the rough Atlantic for the long journey to Europe and the uncertain fate that awaited them.

On each Memorial Day Eve, hundreds of people come together for the annual ritual of the watch fire, sponsored and coordinated by the veterans of Rockland County. The end of the pier opens to its widest point a mile out into the river. We join the crowd gathered safely away from a massive pile of crisscrossed tree logs, some leaning at vertical angles against the main base, like enormous gnarled fingers reaching into the night sky.

The building of the pile has taken a lot of cooperation and hard work by local tree surgeons and landscapers, putting aside some of their biggest specimens log by log. It takes considerable planning and time, all freely given, to transport and then construct the pile.

The volunteer firefighters of Piermont Empire Hose Company No. 1's ladder truck stand at the ready next to their polished red truck. Its emergency lights are flashing, its floodlights illuminating the scene. An extended bucket ladder reaches out over the vast log sculpture.

At the stroke of midnight, following a brief ceremony, the pile is set ablaze to the accompaniment of a cannon's echoing boom. A group of veterans offer a rifle salute. The flames build slowly at first, then grow and leap eagerly at the sky, sparks exploding off the logs and bursting upwards toward the stars. The roaring watch fire illuminates the dark waters of the Hudson River, faintly lighting the land beyond. Its searing heat wafts over us. Some of the veterans stand together watch the rising flames, their faces lit with the memories of lost comrades and past times.

The watch fire is a beacon of remembrance for those seeking its light for direction, pointing the way back toward friendly lines. It is a token of solidarity with the lost patrols that never returned. It is a final blazing tribute to the memory of so many fallen comrades. The fires are tended by veterans and burn through the night until dawn. More great logs are then added to the charred pile and refueled to be set ablaze when darkness falls, to burn through the night once again. Veterans stand watch, changing shifts through the night, and day, and night, the boom of the cannon atop nearby Tallman Mountain joining the hourly rifle shots on the pier. They "give proof through the night" up and down the Hudson River.

Watch fires are as old as our nation, dating back to the Revolutionary War. General Washington used watch fires to signal the cease-fire ending the war for independence, and they are memorialized in the soaring Civil War anthem, "The Battle Hymn of the Republic":

> I have seen Him in the watch fires of a hundred circling camps,
> They have builded Him an altar in the evening dews and damps,
> I can read His righteous sentence by the dim and flaring lamps,
> His day is marching on.

The Rockland County Vietnam Veterans Association revived the tradition of the watch fire in 1987, and many other communities have since taken up the custom. Every Memorial Day, the watch fires light up the sky along the Hudson River, at the sites of some of our nation's earliest and most decisive battles.

The watch fire tradition in Rockland County was the inspiration of a man named Jerry Donnellan. Jerry's idea, executed with tremendous effort, was meant to serve as a mythic calling to the ghosts of veterans past, a fire of warmth and welcome to present veterans, and a promise in the flames that light the dark night to future veterans.

Jerry Donnellan is really something, a big man physically, and maybe an even bigger man spiritually. He also happens to be a real-life war hero.

Back in the jungles of Vietnam, as a sergeant with the 196th Light Infantry Brigade, Jerry and his platoon were fired upon by snipers during a search-and-destroy mission in the Central Highlands. In the middle of a fierce firefight, Jerry got shot in the arm and leg before he and a few of his squad members hurled themselves into a ditch, looking for protection and a chance to return fire. Moments later, a hand grenade was tossed into the ditch beside them. The explosion blew off Jerry's right leg, injured his left leg, and broke his left arm.

During thirteen months in the hospital, doctors managed to save Jerry's left leg, and he was eventually able to return to some semblance of normalcy at his home in Nyack, New York, a river town in the lower Hudson Valley that is the portal to the Tappan Zee Bridge, two miles north of Piermont.

Adjusting back to civilian life was hard for Jerry at first. He didn't know how being an amputee might affect people's opinion of him, but Jerry's drive, intelligence, and personality soon made his disability a nonissue.

Jerry realized how much history surrounded him in his home county. Amid the modern suburban sprawl were visible monuments of our nation's first war—buildings still standing that housed our founding fathers and early soldiers: the DeWint House, where George Washington slept; the Old '76 Tavern, built in 1668 and later used to hang Major Andre, a famous Revolutionary War spy; Brick Church, where the remains of Revolutionary War soldiers rest beneath gravestones whose inscriptions have been worn away by time. Jerry saw his destiny in the legacy of our forefathers, and he has spent his entire adult life making his mark on the area.

In particular, Jerry saw that he had a role in helping others like him who struggled against great odds to become whole again in the aftermath of war. He stepped in to fill a yawning void in veterans' affairs, and his advocacy on their behalf has been nationally recognized. In a 2007 testimony before the House Committee on Veterans' Affairs, Jerry gave a heartfelt statement that brought tears to the eyes of hardened legislators:

> Ever been to war? Mine was in the last century, and that's hard to admit. The fact we lost is even harder. Being shot at tends to focus you, and things experienced stay with you. No one hates war more than those who have lived it, yet we send our children to go and peer into hell. They come back with scars, some physical, more mental. You can't take someone from a normal ordered society and drop them into a combat zone, a year later pull them out, put them back on Main Street, and expect them not to have some baggage. In a strange way the lucky ones with all their fingers and all their toes can carry deeper scars. As scary as it is, you're never more alive than in combat. Your senses are on overload, pores wide open, adrenaline coursing. But you will pay for this dance with the devil, in the silence of a future midnight when the demons return to collect. Old soldiers have passed many such midnights. For us it's normal. The mission is to let this generation know that it can and must be dealt with or it will deal with you. This mission for some has become a career.

Jerry is a fixture in Rockland County. Everyone knows him, and he never hesitates to take a call. I have experienced the depth of his compassion on several occasions when a veteran I knew

needed help or just someone to talk to. If only Jerry could be
cloned a thousand times over, so his bottomless well of love could
be available to men like my brother across the country.

I set out to learn what it means to support the troops, not just in
the frenzied charge to battle, but in the ordinariness that falls
upon veterans like a cloak once they return from the hell of war.

   I have been troubled that for the vast majority of Americans,
the wars in Iraq and Afghanistan only exist in a vague "over there"
kind of way. Unless you have a family member or a friend serving overseas, it is possible to go about your life for days and
weeks on end without sparing a single thought for those who are
serving on our behalf. There are long stretches of time when we
barely hear a word about what is going on far away, in a foreign
land beyond the ocean. We are at war, but you can squint your
eyes just so and not see it. We are at war, but the media focuses
on political game playing, hurricanes, and the latest celebrity hi-
jinks. (Paul Rieckhoff said that when he came home from Iraq, he
was disturbed to find that the media was obsessed with Janet
Jackson's Super Bowl breast fumble. It made him sick.)

   My friend Greg Mitchell, who in his position as editor of *Editor and Publisher* tracks the press coverage of the Iraq War, is disturbed by how faint the whisper has become. "From the lack of
press coverage, you might think the war is over," he says. In the
first half of 2008, newspaper coverage of the war fell to 3 percent
of the stories; on cable news it was worse, a paltry 1 percent. It's
a scathing indictment not only of the press, but of a citizenry that
would rather not know.

   As the war in Iraq has dragged on, circumstances for journalists have become more difficult. The media presence on the
ground in Iraq is a fraction of its former might. Major networks
like CBS and NBC don't even have full-time journalists covering
the war anymore. The military has grown increasingly reluctant

to embed them, due to a combination of security concerns and, frankly, an effort to prevent the worst pictures of the war from receiving mainstream viewing. In September 2007, there were 219 embedded journalists. In September 2008, there were only thirty-nine.

I have heard editors defend their lack of coverage by saying that they're in the business of selling newspapers, and that means giving more space to lifestyle features that draw readership. But as Greg Mitchell often points out, the press has a larger mission than simply following the public into a trough, where it feeds on denial and distraction. The press also has a responsibility to educate the public, to give them access to information, solid reportage, and clarifying analysis.

Susan Tifft, professor of journalism and public policy at Duke University, points out that it is common for the public, and even journalists themselves, to develop an immunity to violence when it is played out year after year. "Somehow we have gotten used to it," she says. "That's why it seems like wallpaper or Muzak. It's oddly normal and just part of the atmosphere."

Although we live in the most media-saturated time in history, we rarely see photos or footage of the battlefields. The wars in Afghanistan and Iraq have seemed oddly sanitized. Until the 2007 revelations about the dire conditions at Walter Reed Army Medical Center, little was heard about the thousands of wounded soldiers who, to this day, languish in veterans' hospitals, suffering severe brain injuries, missing limbs, or burned beyond recognition. Now that the initial flurry of publicity has passed, most of these wounded vets have sunk back into their real world—the twenty-four-hour, seven-days-a-week world of pain, isolation, and anonymity. We don't bear witness to their shrapnel-shattered faces or mangled lives. For the most part, unless you're a friend or relative, you don't even know who they are. The Pentagon lists only the dead among the casualties of war. The names of soldiers wounded in action are not published in casualty postings from the U.S. Central Command or the Pentagon, and their numbers are only divulged when they are specifically requested by a media organization. Current estimates count the wounded in Iraq at a modest 31,000, but that number excludes thousands of others who have suffered noncombat-related injuries or illnesses.

Even the dead are kept at a discreet distance. There is a media blackout at Dover Air Force Base in Delaware, where the bodies of soldiers killed in action arrive on enormous C-130 cargo planes, and are unceremoniously disembarked from the aircraft in the dark of night. The aluminum cases that hold the decedents' remains are no longer known as "body bags," as they were in Nam, or "human remains pouches," the moniker employed during the Gulf War. The Pentagon now officially refers to the aluminum cases as "transfer tubes"—a term meant to whitewash the terrible stain that is death.

So who will care? Let's begin with those who already *do* care, not just with words, but with actions. When it comes to walking the walk in support of the troops—on the battlefield and here at home—one group of people deserves high praise: the veterans themselves. I have been repeatedly impressed by the way veterans rush to help others in need. And I'm not just talking about activist veterans, but also the ordinary guys who answer the call again and again. When I was reading the message boards, unit pages, and Web sites where veterans communicate with one another, there were frequent postings: "A brother needs our help." The circumstances might be a need for money, help filing a claim, or just a phone call to say hello. And the brothers responded. It didn't matter if they knew the person in trouble.

In one instance, a Vietnam veteran, who had served with the 199th Light Infantry Brigade, had been incarcerated, and money for his defense was raised on the Internet. As one of his supporters, a man who did not personally know him, wrote with such abiding love and regard:

> I know of no better group of men than you guys. Someone once said, "Those who served in our war from our generation were not the best and brightest." I say not only that you guys are the best and brightest, but we all shared a defining time that gave us a brotherhood second to none and those who will drive hundreds of miles to be beside you in times of need. When my wife passed away I had friends drive and show up, call and ask if I needed them, sent her the flowers she loved. Some stayed on watch to keep me from leaving. I read these posts from men I did not personally know but hold a personal love for them as my brothers. It is who we are. Let us remain the best of all, let us remain compassionate and caring, let us remain loyal to each other. I add my prayer with my brothers. May God Bless each and all.

The words from "America the Beautiful," "crown thy good with brotherhood"—come to mind when I think of these faithful comrades. For the most part, they are civilians who laid down their arms long ago, but they are determined not to leave their comrades behind. They have something to teach us all about valor and loyalty.

Perhaps you've seen them roaring down the highway, hundreds strong, on their motorcycles, the insignia POW/MIA emblazoned on their leather jackets and on the orange and black flags fluttering from their handlebars.

Perhaps you've encountered them at AA meetings or in church pews, always ready with a helping hand.

Perhaps you've seen them behind the wheels of cars that bear a dozen bumper stickers: "Support the Troops," "Vietnam Veteran," "Proud Iraq Veteran," "God Bless America."

Perhaps you've seen them making a difference in a thousand ways, great and small. They embody a code of brotherhood. They never forget. They keep the watch fires burning.

The veterans I know were, like my brother, pure patriots, proud to serve. But even among those who have done well in life, there is a sense of demoralization that they have never been able to shake. Faced with the question of what to do with the rest of their lives, they made one of several choices: seeking lives of achievement in the civilian world, remaining in the military, or dropping out of society. Some have straddled two worlds, forming strong but unconventional bonds with the brethren. For example, my friend Jay, a very successful photographer and businessman in the "regular" world, lives an alternative life as an active member of the Nam Knights and a part of Rolling Thunder, a large group of veteran bikers. Jay is a handsome, tall, slender man, with a flowing beard and blazing eyes, whose activism is not about the past. He takes the promise "Never again" with the utmost seriousness, and his current mission is to make sure that the young soldiers wounded in Afghanistan and Iraq are getting their just desserts from the military. "We try to get into Walter Reed and talk to the guys—make sure they get their benefits applications filled out," he says. "Those applications are a mother. I know guys from Nam who couldn't deal with the paperwork, and never got a cent. Problem is, they've tried to block us from seeing the guys—say it's a national security issue."

The annual Rolling Thunder rally in Washington, D.C., over the Memorial Day weekend, is an important time for Jay. It's his private reunion, a special world where outsiders are not welcome. When I asked if I could accompany him one year, his normally friendly face shut down. This was a line that could not be crossed. "I don't think there would be anything for you to see," he mumbled. "You know, it's just us talking, being together." Jay revels in the annual ritual of Rolling Thunder, but it takes a toll. The weeks after Memorial Day every year find him in quiet retreat, chasing ghosts.

As much as the support of the brotherhood means to these men and women, it is the respect of ordinary civilians that can be transformational for them. A Vietnam veteran told me this story: He had struggled for many years to put the war behind him and had been mostly successful. But the thing that really ate at him was the harsh way he and his fellow soldiers were treated when they came home from Vietnam. He'd never been able to shake his bitterness about that. One day, not long ago, he was at the supermarket loading groceries into his car. A woman passing by saw his bumper sticker, "Vietnam War Veteran," and she paused to say, "Thank you for your service." He choked up with emotion, and could barely describe the warming effect of her simple gesture.

Keeping soldiers and veterans at the forefront of the American consciousness is like skipping stones across a river. They create a ripple, strong and wide, when they drop, but soon the surface of the water returns to its glassy calm.

One such stone was a feature in February 2007 by *Washington Post* reporters Dana Priest and Anne Hull exposing the despicable conditions at the Walter Reed Army Medical Center's outpatient unit. There was an outcry.

A second stone was a report that seriously wounded soldiers in military hospitals were being charged for food, toilet paper, and other essentials. There was an outcry.

A third stone was a YouTube video by the father of a soldier returning from Afghanistan, showing the filthy, crumbling barracks at Fort Bragg that were to serve as his unit's housing. There was an outcry.

But all too soon after the stones dropped, the waters cleared, the waves disappeared, and the still surface of America's consciousness was restored. Life went on, and the river showed no sign that there had ever been a ripple.

In one of my conversations with my brother's friend Bill, he revealed that he'd often tried to get Jim to talk about his family, but Jim always shut down. "You were the only one he said he got along with," Bill said.

"Me?" I gasped, thinking he'd got it wrong. "I'm sure Jim wasn't talking about me," I said. "Maybe one of my sisters."

"No," he insisted. "I'm sure it was you. His sister in New York. He mentioned all the crazy stuff you did together when you were kids. He talked about you so fondly."

"Oh." I was struck silent by this revelation. I felt tears itching at the backs of my eyes. I gulped. "Why didn't he get in touch with me?" I asked finally, my voice shaking.

"I don't know. I think he said he tried once . . ."

That call.

I chastised myself—how could I not? There had been many mysteries in Jim's life, but the one thing I thought I knew for certain was that he couldn't stand me. I returned the favor, deciding I couldn't stand him either. We both lost out, but mine was the deeper shame. I was in a better position to reach out, and I chose not to. And it *was* a choice. Oh, I piled on the excuses over the years, like sandbags loaded around the exteriors of the bunkers at forward operating bases in a war zone. I was engaged in self-defense, guarding against the incoming fire of ideas and truths I couldn't understand or stomach.

At that moment, I finally understood why I needed to write this book. Supporting the troops begins in our hearts. It is grounded in our convictions and then proven by our actions. It is molded from compassion and charity, the willingness to look into the eyes of someone who seems a stranger, and say, "You are my brother. We are alike." It is a practical demonstration of kinship.

=====

On a recent Saturday morning, I approached the intersection at Route 59 and Middletown Road, as I had done on hundreds of occasions, but this time I felt new resolve. The groups were there, ever loyal to their causes: on the near corner, "Honk to support the troops," and on the far corner, "Honk for peace." For the first time ever, I pressed my hand to the steering wheel, honking to support the troops. "For you, Jim," I said out loud. And then, as I crossed over to the other side, I pressed my horn again, for peace. "For you, Jim," I said again. It felt right to break my silence after all those years. And yet, these were still slogans, incapable of communicating true resolve, much less offering either support or peace. I did it just that once, as a symbolic gesture.

The truth about war and peace, about living in community, about loving a nation and one another, is that our world is a treacherous landscape where each choice is complex, and each behavior heavy with consequence. Our sins against one another are many. Yet every day we have a fresh opportunity to open our hearts and to reach out a hand, in a way that only humans can, and say, "You are my brother . . . You are my sister . . . We are alike."

DEAR
BROTHER

Dear Jim,

Greg called the other day. He said he thought I should let you rest in peace. It got to me, his saying that. I wondered if he was right. Stirring up old stuff has never been our family's way. Remember when we were kids and nobody told us how Dad's father died, or why Mom's dad was sick for so many years? They were just mysteries. The way of our world was so cut-and-dried then. The dead were gone, outside the reach of our concerns. What was the point of finding out truths that couldn't be remedied?

Considering that you spent so many years in hiding, I think Greg believes that it's not respectful for me to be poking around in your life, and it's not what you would have wanted. But I have chosen to see it another way. Your life and service meant something, and your story, in a strange way, is like a beacon for others, although there are many sad parts. The light of your life flickered on and off, but yours is a common story among veterans. I think you—and they—should be honored, not blamed.

Would it ease your mind to know that I think about you every day? I guess you'd be within your rights to say it's a little late.

Sometimes I wonder if I'm being self-indulgent at your expense. After all, I didn't care so much when my caring might have helped you. Has this all been an exercise in making myself feel better, trying to even the score and justify my own negligence? I hope not, because I want it to be more.

I'll bet you'd smile a little to know that your sister has written about you, that your picture is on the cover of a book. I remember when that picture was taken. You were nineteen, on your second tour in Vietnam. You went to some photo shop in Saigon, and mailed the print home to Mom. God, you were handsome! But your eyes seem a thousand years old. What were you thinking that day?

Maybe you'd like to hear that we all shed tears for you. We talk about you at family gatherings. We miss you, and I know you missed us during all those years of silence. Your friends from Texas also think about you. You live on in their memories as a good person, a dear man.

I spoke with one of your old buddies the other day. He was with you in the pit in Vietnam, when you were both only eighteen years old. He said that anyone who claimed they weren't scared shitless over there would be lying, but he also said that in a strange way he'd never been happier than he was then. He said you were a good motherfucker—his words. I'll bet you were.

The greatest disservice I did you was not to be proud of you. I owed you that, and I'm sorry I couldn't have done a better job of it. When I think about you now, I consider all the men you saved by your actions in combat, the burdens you eased, the lives you made possible. You and I were in our own kind of combat through all of those years. But that was only a small piece of it. You were looking not just for the thanks of a grateful nation, but for the respect of a grateful family, and we failed you. That being said, it gives me comfort to realize that somewhere out there in this vast nation, a man is sitting on his deck, enjoying the view, who would not be alive today except for you.

The time for a reckoning about our mutual failures is long past. While I don't have Mom's certain faith that we'll all be reunited in the hereafter, a part of me hopes it's true and I will see you again. Until then, I'm going to let you go. Rest in peace, brother.

Love,

Catherine

RESOURCES FOR VETERANS

THE GOOD NEWS is that there are hundreds of organizations and support groups serving veterans. However, it can be difficult to navigate the universe of veterans' sites. In an effort to highlight those that are most popular or that address the most pressing needs of veterans, I have selected the following resources. As you browse these Web sites, you will find additional links. There are a lot of people out there trying to help.

In these pages, you will find listings in the following areas:

General Information, Support, Advocacy
Political Action Committees
Benefits/Filing Claims
Post-Traumatic Stress Disorder Support
Help for Disabled Veterans
Housing/Employment Support
Support for Families of Veterans
POW/MIA Information and Support
Agent Orange/Gulf War Syndrome
Military Buddy Search
Antiwar Activism in the Military
Government Support for Veterans
Veteran Record Search
Veterans Bookshelf

General Information, Support, Advocacy

- **American Legion** (www.legion.org): A patriotic, nonprofit, wartime veterans' organization devoted to mutual helpfulness.
- **AMVETS** (www.amvets.org): A volunteer-led organization formed by World War II veterans that provides not only support for veterans and the active military in procuring their earned entitlements, but also community services that enhance the quality of life for veterans.
- **Gulf War Veteran Resource Pages** (www.gulfweb.org): A volunteer-operated site that supports Gulf War veterans, especially regarding claims and medical support.
- **Iraq and Afghanistan Veterans of America** (www.iava.org): The nation's first and largest group dedicated to the troops and veterans of the wars in Iraq and Afghanistan, and the civilian supporters of those troops and veterans. (This is the organization started by Paul Rieckhoff, whose work is described in chapter 8.)
- **Iraq War Veterans Organization** (www.iraqwarveterans.org): Provides information and support for Operation Iraqi Freedom veterans, Global War on Terror veterans, Operation Enduring Freedom veterans, active military personnel and family members related to pre-deployment, deployment, and post-deployment issues, as well as information about PTSD, health issues, and veterans benefits.
- **National Veterans Foundation** (www.nvf.org): Serves the crisis management, information, and referral needs of all U.S. veterans and their families. NVF also operates the nation's only toll-free hotline for veterans and their families.
- **United Female Veterans of America** (www.ufva.us): An organization that supports women who have served in the military.
- **Veterans for America** (www.veteransforamerica.org): An advocacy and humanitarian organization whose goal is to ensure that our country meets the needs of service members and veterans who have served in Operation Enduring Freedom and Operation Iraqi Freedom. VFA focuses specifically on the signature wounds of these conflicts: psychological traumas and traumatic brain injuries.
- **Veterans of Foreign Wars** (www.vfw.org): An organization that supports veterans who served overseas and deployed service members.
- **Veterans Network** (www.veteransnetwork.net): An online radio and TV network for veterans that explores issues and legislation, and offers education and resources of interest to veterans.

- **Vietnam Veterans** (www.vietvet.org): A personal, reader-friendly page with reflections, information, and support by and for veterans of the Vietnam War.
- **Vietnam Veterans of America** (www.vva.org): Founded in 1978, the VVA is dedicated to Vietnam-era veterans and their families.
- **VietNow** (www.vietnow.com): A personal support organization for veterans and their families.

Political Action Committees
- **Circle of Friends for American Veterans** (www.vetsvision.org): A 501(c)(3) organization dedicated to influencing public opinion and affecting public policy in support of homeless veterans.
- **Veterans' Alliance for Security and Democracy (VETPAC)** (www.vetpac.org): A multicandidate political action committee that endorses, actively supports, and helps fund candidates for national office (who are sometimes, but not always, veterans).

Benefits/Filing Claims
- **National Veterans Organization Information Service** (www.nvo.org): A not-for-profit corporation chartered by the state of Delaware, dedicated to the preservation and enhancement of veterans benefits. NVO is composed mostly of disabled veterans who are tired of the way that veterans are treated by the U.S. Department of Veterans Affairs and the U.S. Congress.
- **GI Bill 2008** (www.GIBill2008.org): Tools and guidelines to help veterans take full advantage of the new GI Bill.

Post-Traumatic Stress Disorder Support
- **Disabled American Veterans** (www.dav.org): Provides free assistance to veterans in obtaining benefits and services earned through their military service.
- **Invisible Wounds of War Study** (www.rand.org/multi/military/veterans/): A RAND Corporation project that assesses the post-deployment health-related needs associated with post-traumatic stress disorder, major depression, and traumatic brain injury; examines the treatment capacity of the current health care system; and estimates the costs of providing quality health care to all military members who need it.
- **National Center for Post-Traumatic Stress Disorder** (www.ncptsd.org): A program of the VA, dedicated to research and education on the prevention, understanding, and treatment of PTSD.

- **National Suicide Prevention Lifeline** (www.suicidepreventionlife line.org): A twenty-four-hour, toll-free suicide prevention service available to anyone in suicidal crisis that includes a new service for veterans. Call 1-800-273-8255 and press 1 to be connected immediately to VA suicide prevention and mental health service professionals.
- **Post-Traumatic Gazette** (http://patiencepress.com/ptg.html): A newsletter providing a healing perspective for all trauma survivors, their families, friends, and therapists. Contact Patience Mason, editor and publisher: PO Box 2757, High Springs, FL 32655-2757; phone: 386-454-1651; e-mail: tg@patiencepress.com.

Help for Disabled Veterans

- **Paralyzed Veterans of America** (www.pva.org): An organization that works to maximize the quality of life for its members and all people with SCI/D through research, education, and the pursuit of veterans' benefits and rights, accessibility and the removal of architectural barriers, sports programs, and disability rights.
- **Stand Up For Veterans** (www.standup4vets.org): An initiative of Disabled American Veterans devoted to finding public policy solutions for all veterans, especially those returning from Afghanistan or Iraq who suffer devastating injuries and disabilities, including traumatic brain injury and post-traumatic stress disorder.
- **Wounded Warrior Project** (www.woundedwarriorproject.org): Provides tangible support to the severely wounded, helping them on the road to physical and emotional health.

Housing/Employment Support

- **Hire Vets First** (www.hirevetsfirst.gov): A comprehensive career Web site for managers, human resources professionals, and veterans that encourages hiring veterans of America's military.
- **National Coalition for Homeless Veterans** (www.nchv.org): A nonprofit organization that serves as a resource and technical assistance center for a national network of community-based service providers and local, state, and federal agencies that provide emergency and supportive housing, food, health services, job training and placement assistance, legal aid, and case-management support for homeless veterans.
- **Stand Down** (www.va.gov/homeless): Part of the Department of Veterans Affairs' efforts to provide services to homeless veterans. Stand Downs are typically one-to three-day events providing homeless veterans with services including food, shelter, clothing,

health screenings, VA and Social Security benefits counseling, and referrals to a variety of other necessary services, such as housing, employment, and substance abuse treatment.

Support for Families of Veterans

- **American Gold Star Mothers** (www.goldstarmoms.com): A support and advocacy group for mothers of men and women killed in war.
- **Daughters of Vietnam Veterans** (www.dovv.net): Support, information, a newsletter, and a loving space for children of Vietnam veterans.
- **Operation Homefront** (www.operationhomefront.net): Provides emergency assistance and morale to the troops and the families they leave behind, and to wounded warriors when they return home.
- **Sanctuary for Veterans & Families** (www.sanctuaryvf.org): An organization that promotes healthier, more resilient military families by providing direct support, services, and advocacy, addressing the impacts of combat-related trauma, and facilitating the reintegration of veterans into the family system and community.
- **Veterans and Families** (www.veteransandfamilies.org): A non-profit community service and support organization, founded and directed by veterans, parents, grandparents, family members, employers, mental health professionals, academics, philanthropists, and community leaders, with a mission to assist veterans and their families to successfully transition home from deployment.
- **Vietnam Veterans Memorial** (www.thewall-usa.com): A Web site dedicated to honoring those who died in the Vietnam War, and a healing place for their families.
- **Vietnam Veteran Wives** (www.vietnamveteranwives.org): A support network for the families of veterans.

POW/MIA Information and Support

- **American Ex-Prisoners of War** (www.axpow.org): A national organization for American citizens who were captured by the enemy. Membership is open to all former prisoners of war from any theater in any war, all former civilian internees, and to their families.
- **Rolling Thunder** (www.rollingthunder1.com): A motorcycle community that publicizes POW/MIA issues, and educates the public about the many American prisoners of war who were left behind in war.

Agent Orange/Gulf War Syndrome

While there is a tremendous amount of information about Agent Orange and
Gulf War syndrome on the general Web sites listed above, as well as on the VA
sites, the following are sites specially dedicated to these topics.

- **Agent Orange Quilt of Tears** (www.agentorangequiltoftears.com):
  A memorial and support group for victims of Agent Orange.
  (This is the quilting society started by Jennie Le Favre and described in chapter 8.)
- **Agent Orange Widows Awareness Coalition** (www.aowac.org):
  Devoted to locating veterans who served in Vietnam from 1962
  to 1975 and informing them of the diseases and health risks
  associated with military service, to veterans, their postwar children, and families. This group also supports veterans who served
  in Korea in 1968 and 1969, and other veterans who may have
  been exposed to Agent Orange and other herbicides and chemicals while on military service elsewhere during the testing,
  transporting, or spraying of herbicides for military purposes.
- **American Gulf War Veterans Association** (www.gulfwarvets.com):
  A site emphasizing information and support for veterans with
  Gulf War syndrome.

Military Buddy Search

The best way to start a military buddy search is to look for your former battalion or company online. Many of them have dedicated Web sites or Yahoo!
groups. Here are some other suggestions:

- **Lost and the Found** (http://grunt.space.swri.edu/lostfnd.htm): A
  Web locator for veterans and friends of veterans who are looking for other Vietnam veterans.
- **Military.com** (www.military.com): Unit pages and a search facility for military buddies from past and current wars. A subcate-
  gory of this massive site is www.armylocator.com.
- **VetFriends.com** (www.vetfriends.com): Helps veterans reunite
  with friends and family who are veterans of or are currently serving in all branches of the military.

Antiwar Activism in the Military

- **Iraq Veterans Against the War** (www.ivaw.org): Organized to give
  a voice to the large number of active-duty service people and
  veterans who are against the Iraq War but who are under various pressures to remain silent.
- **Veterans for Peace** (www.veteransforpeace.org): A network of veterans working together for peace and justice around the world.

- **Vietnam Veterans Against the War** (www.vvawai.org): Supports the protest of American intervention overseas. Started during the Vietnam War, this organization has expanded its charter to be a force against all wars.

Government Support for Veterans

- **United States Department of Veterans Affairs** (www.va.gov): The government Web site is a comprehensive resource for all veteran information. Be warned: the bureaucratic enormity of the VA can be intimidating. Before tackling the VA, I recommend visiting one of the private veterans support groups listed above.

The government Web site contains the following services:
VA Facilities Directory
VA Forms
VA Publications
VA General Counsel Opinions
Gulf War Veterans' Illnesses
National Center for Post-Traumatic Stress Disorder (PTSD)
Women Veterans Issues

VETERANS BENEFITS ADMINISTRATION
VBA Compensation and Pension Service
VBA Vocational Rehabilitation and Employment Service (VR&E)
VBA Home Loan Guarantee Service
VBA Life Insurance Service
VBA Education Service
VA Survivor Benefits
VA Benefit Rate Tables
List of Veterans Affairs Medical Centers by State

VETERANS HEALTH ADMINISTRATION (VHA)
VHA Health Care Eligibility
VHA C&P Examination Worksheets
VHA CARES Program
VHA Foreign Medical Program
VHA CHAMPVA (Civilian Health and Medical Program of the
   Department of Veterans Affairs)

Veterans Record Search
If you need a copy of your records or the records of a relative, you can download forms from the VA Web site, and send them to:

National Personnel Records Center
Military Personnel
9700 Page Avenue
St. Louis, MO
63132-5100

Note that under the provisions of the Privacy Act of 1974, applicants must have the written consent of the individual whose records are involved before a request is considered. If the applicant is a minor dependent of a veteran, the parent or legal guardian must sign the release. If the applicant is mentally incompetent, the legal guardian must sign the release. (The legal representative or guardian must also furnish a copy of the court appointment.)

The Privacy Act of 1974 also provides for the release of information with the written consent of the individual to whom the records pertain. The Privacy Act does not apply to the records of deceased individuals. However, Department of Defense instructions indicate that in such cases there must be written consent of the next of kin. For purposes of release, the next of kin is defined as any of the following: unremarried widow or widower, son, daughter, father, mother, brother, or sister.

For more information, call the customer service center at 314-801-0800.

Veterans Bookshelf

Hundreds of books have been written about the military. This selection represents my favorites, and those I found most helpful in addressing some of the issues covered in this book. I have included a few titles that may no longer be front and center on the shelves of your local bookstore. But all books listed here are available new or used on Amazon.com.

WORLD WAR I AND II/KOREAN WAR

The Bonus Army: An American Epic by Paul Dickson and Thomas B. Allen (Walker and Co., 2006).

Flags of Our Fathers by James Bradley and Ron Powers (Gale Group, 2000).

Our Fathers' War: Growing Up in the Shadow of the Greatest Generation by Tom Mathews (Broadway Books, 2005).

VIETNAM WAR

If Morning Never Comes by Bill VandenBush (The Old Hundred and One Press, 2003).

Long Time Passing: Vietnam and the Haunted Generation by Myra MacPherson (Doubleday, 1984).

Reminds Me of the Time: Vietnam 1968 by A. Edward Wade (Infinity Publishing, 2004).

Shadows of a Vietnam Veteran: Silent Victims by Alicia J. Boyd (Truman Publishing, 2001).

"These Are My Credentials": The 199th Light Infantry Brigade in the Republic of Vietnam 1966–1970 by Robert J. Gouge (AuthorHouse, 2004).

The Things They Carried by Tim O'Brien (paperback, Broadway Books 1998).

Touring Nam: Vietnam War Stories edited by Martin H. Greenberg and Augustus Richard Norton (Quill/William Morrow, 1985).

Tour of Duty: John Kerry and the Vietnam War by Douglas Brinkley (William Morrow, 2004).

Vietnam Order of Battle: A Complete Illustrated Reference to U.S. Army Combat Support Forces in Vietnam 1961–1973 by Captain Shelby L. Stanton (Stackpole Books, 2003).

The Vietnam War Almanac by Harry G. Summers Jr. (Presidio Press, 1999).

We Are Soldiers Still: A Journey Back to the Battlefields of Vietnam by Harold G. Moore and Joseph L. Galloway (HarperCollins, 2008).

We Were Soldiers . . . and Young: Ia Drang—the Battle That Changed the War in Vietnam by Harold G. Moore and Joseph L. Galloway (Presidio Press, 2004).

Why Vietnam Matters: An Eyewitness Account of Lessons Not Learned by Rufus Phillips (Naval Institute Press, 2008).

Working-Class War: American Combat Soldiers and Vietnam by Christian G. Appy (University of North Carolina Press, 1993).

GULF WAR/AFGHANISTAN AND IRAQ WARS

Baghdad at Sunrise: A Brigade Commander's War in Iraq by Peter R. Mansoor (Yale University Press, 2008).

Chasing Ghosts: Failures and Facades in Iraq: A Soldier's Perspective by Paul Rieckhoff (NAL, 2007).

In Conflict: Iraq War Veterans Speak Out on Duty, Loss, and the Fight to Stay Alive by Yvonne Latty (Polipoint Press, 2006).

Iraq and the Lessons of Vietnam: Or, How Not to Learn from the Past by Lloyd C. Gardner and Marilyn B. Young (New Press, 2008).

Jarhead: A Marine's Chronicle of the Gulf War and Other Battles by Anthony Swofford (Scribner, 2003).

The Long Road Home: A Story of War and Family by Martha Raddatz (Putnam, 2007).

Made a Difference for That One: A Surgeon's Letters Home from Iraq compiled by Meredith Coffala (iUniverse, 2005).

So Wrong For So Long: How the Press, the Pundits—and the President—Failed in Iraq by Greg Mitchell (Union Square Press, 2008).

Two Wars: One Hero's Fight on Two Fronts; Abroad and Within by Nate Self (Tyndale House, 2008).

What Was Asked of Us: An Oral History of the Iraq War by the Soldiers Who Fought It by Trish Wood (Little, Brown, 2006).

VETERANS ISSUES

Flashback: Posttraumatic Stress Disorder, Suicide, and the Lessons of War by Penny Coleman (Beacon Press, 2007).

For Service to Your Country: The Insider's Guide to Veterans' Benefits by Peter S. Gaytan and Marian Edelman Borden (Citadel, 2008).

Growing Up Empty: The Hunger Epidemic in America by Loretta Schwartz-Nobel (HarperCollins, 2002).

Heroes at Home: Help and Hope for America's Military Families by Ellie Kay (Bethany House, 2002).

In An Instant: A Family's Journey of Love and Healing by Lee and Bob Woodruff (Random House, 2007).

Nickel and Dimed: On (Not) Getting By in America by Barbara Ehrenreich (Henry Holt, 2002).

Odysseus in America: Combat Trauma and the Trials of Homecoming by Jonathan Shay (Scribner, 2003).

Uncle Sam's Shame: Inside Our Broken Veterans Administration by Martin Kantor (Praeger Security International, 2008).

Veterans of War, Veterans of Peace edited by Maxine Hong Kingston (Koa Books, 2006).

The Veteran's Survival Guide: How to File and Collect on VA Claims, 2nd ed., by John D. Roche (Potomac Books, 2006).

Veterans Unclaimed Benefits: The Insider's Guide by Michael Riedel (Author-House, 2005).

Vets Under Siege: How America Deceives and Dishonors Those Who Fight Our Battles by Martin Schram (Thomas Dunne Books/St. Martin's Press, 2008).

War and the Soul: Healing Our Nation's Veterans from Post-Traumatic Stress Disorder by Edward Tick (Quest Books, 2005).

THE PSYCHOLOGY OF WAR

Achilles in Vietnam: Combat Trauma and the Undoing of Character by Jonathan Shay (Scribner, 1994).

No More Heroes: Madness and Psychiatry in War by Richard A. Gabriel (Hill and Wang, 1988).

On Combat: The Psychology and Physiology of Deadly Conflict in War and in Peace by Lt. Col. Dave Grossman with Loren W. Christensen (Warrior Science Publications, 2004).

On Killing: The Psychological Cost of Learning to Kill in War and Society by Lt. Col. Dave Grossman (Little, Brown, 1995).

The Psychology of War: Comprehending Its Mystique and Its Madness by Lawrence LeShan (Helios Press, 2002).

War Is a Force That Gives Us Meaning by Chris Hedges (PublicAffairs, 2002).

NOTES

——

Military Veterans: General Statistics

These are the most current statistics provided by the Census Bureau concerning the demographics of military veterans. As of the last Census Bureau update in 2006, there were 23.7 million vets in the United States. The breakdown is as follows:

FEMALES

There are 1.7 million female veterans. Of these, 16 percent are veterans of the Gulf War.

ETHNIC MAKEUP OR ORIGIN

There are 2.4 million black veterans, 1.1 million Hispanic veterans, 292,000 Asian veterans, 169,000 American Indian or Alaska Native veterans, and 28,000 Native Hawaiian or other Pacific Islander veterans.

AGE

There are 9.2 million veterans age sixty-five and older; at the other end of the age spectrum, 1.9 million are younger than thirty-five.

WHERE THEY SERVED

There are 8 million Vietnam-era veterans, accounting for 33 percent of all living veterans. There are 4.6 Gulf War veterans (representing service from August 2, 1990, to the present); 3.2 million World War II veterans; 3.1 million Korean War veterans; and 6.1 million peacetime veterans.

There are 430,000 living veterans who served during both the Vietnam War and the Gulf War. There are other living veterans who served in two or more wars. These include: 350,000 who served during both the Korean and Vietnam wars; 78,000 who served during three conflicts—World War II, the Korean War, and the Vietnam War; and 294,000 who served in both World War II and the Korean War. There are three documented living World War I veterans.

2. An Army of Youth

27 Tom Mathews, author of *Our Fathers' War* (Broadway Books, 2005), worked for three decades for *Newsweek*, where he served as New York bureau chief, senior writer for national affairs, foreign editor, culture editor, and senior editor for special projects, and won a National Magazine Award. For the past ten years, Mathews has written or coauthored several works about soldiers and war.

28 The My Lai massacre epitomized the dehumanization of the enemy during the Vietnam War. The massacre was waged by U.S. Army forces on March 16, 1968, in the hamlets of My Lai and My Khe, and resulted in the brutal deaths of between 347 and 504 unarmed citizens, many of them women, children, and elderly men. The motivation for the assault was the conviction on the part of the officers that the hamlets were harboring Vietcong, although this turned out not to be true. Under the command of Lt. William Calley, troops of Charlie Company, the Eleventh Brigade, went on a killing spree that was fueled by anger, revenge, frustration, and a wild, unstoppable fury. As reported by the BBC: "Soldiers went berserk, gunning down unarmed men, women, children and babies. Families which huddled together for safety in huts or bunkers were shown no mercy. Those who emerged with hands held high were murdered . . . Elsewhere in the village, other atrocities were in progress. Women were gang raped; Vietnamese who had bowed to greet the Americans were beaten with fists and tortured, clubbed with rifle butts and stabbed with bayonets. Some victims were mutilated with the signature 'C Company' carved into the chest. By late morning word had got back to higher authorities and a ceasefire was ordered. My Lai was in a state of carnage. Bodies were strewn through the village. Some of the victims were sexually abused, beaten, tortured, or maimed, and some of the bodies were found mutilated."

Later, twenty-six soldiers would face criminal charges for their actions, but only Calley was convicted. He served four and one-half months of his two-year sentence.

31 Bishop Fulton J. Sheen was such an outspoken voice against the evils of Communism that it came as a shock when he opposed the Vietnam War in his final years. However, even Bishop Sheen's seemingly pro-war writings were rigorous in parsing the necessity of war in what could be considered moral terms. Of particular note is his essay, "Conditions of a Just War," written in 1940, as the world was struggling to respond to Hitler's aggression.

33 Jerry Lembcke was a U.S. Army chaplain's assistant in Vietnam. He is now associate professor of sociology at Holy Cross College in Worcester, Massachusetts, and the author of *The Spitting Image: Myth, Memory, and the Legacy of Vietnam* (NYU Press, 2000).

34 On April 24, 2007, the House Oversight and Government Reform Committee, chaired by California Democrat Henry Waxman, held a hearing to

examine the false stories spread about Jessica Lynch and Pat Tillman. The hearing yielded little result, but was notable for Lynch's testimony. In part, Lynch stated: "My parents' home in Wirt County was under siege of the media all repeating the story of the little girl Rambo from the hills who went down fighting. It was not true. I have repeatedly said, when asked, that if the stories about me helped inspire our troops and rally a nation, then perhaps there was some good. However, I am still confused as to why they chose to lie and tried to make me a legend when the real heroics of my fellow soldiers that day were, in fact, legendary. People like Lori Piestewa and First Sergeant Dowdy who picked up fellow soldiers in harm's way. Or people like Patrick Miller and Sergeant Donald Walters who actually fought until the very end. The bottom line is the American people are capable of determining their own ideals for heroes and they don't need to be told elaborate tales."

3. Jim's War

41 According to data compiled by the Army Recruiting Command in Fort Knox, Kentucky, the period during the Afghanistan and Iraq wars has been marked by a troubling decline in the quality of recruits. Over 40 percent of army recruits in 2006 and 2007 had below-average verbal and math scores on the Armed Forces Qualification Test, compared to 28.9 percent in 2003. Nearly 20 percent did not have high-school diplomas, compared to 10 percent prior to the Iraq War.

42 Boot camp has been a frequent subject of movies and plays. For the Vietnam era, two stand out. *Full Metal Jacket* is a 1987 Stanley Kubrick film, based on the novel *The Short-Timers* by Gustav Hasford. The first half of the film takes place during Marine Corps basic training at Parris Island, where a brutal drill sergeant generates a survival-of-the-fittest madness among the new recruits, ending in a horrifying murder-suicide. The film was nominated for an Oscar. *The Basic Training of Pavlo Hummel*, a play by David Rabe, follows the fate of a mentally disturbed army recruit whose mind is further warped by basic training, and whose senseless death (mindlessly grabbing a live grenade in a Saigon brothel) is a sad but predictable denouement. *Full Metal Jacket* and *The Basic Training of Pavlo Hummel* both demonstrate the vulnerability of military recruits, especially those who are not suited to the discipline or mental cohesion required for war.

44 "Boot Camp Violence: Abuse in Vietnam War-Era Basic Training" is a 1995 study conducted by Brandon Johnson and Robert A. Goldberg, Department of History, University of Utah. The abstract reads: "Abuse of recruits was a significant element of the United States military's basic training in the Vietnam War era. Many contemporary scholars argue that 'boot camp' mistreatment contributed heavily to the violence practiced by many American soldiers in Vietnam."

50   The First Engineer Battalion, known as the Diehard Engineers, hosts an excellent Web site, www.diehardengineer.com, filled with historical documents, photographs, and reflections from the Vietnam War.

51   "U.S. Army Engineers 1965–1970" is a highly detailed account of the work of the army engineers in Vietnam by Maj. Gen. Robert R. Ploger, Department of the Army. The full document is available online. According to Major Ploger, "The doctrinal mission of an engineer battalion organic to a division is to increase the combat effectiveness of the division by performing various engineer tasks and, when necessary, fighting as infantry. To use other terms, the mission of the divisional engineers in Vietnam was to improve the mobility of friendly forces and to impede the mobility of the enemy. Their specialized skills and equipment were often of vital importance in sustaining the impetus of an offensive operation carried out by U.S. and allied troops. Engineer demolition teams were frequently called upon in combat operations to destroy enemy base camps, material, and tunnels. Divisional engineer battalions often designated one of their subordinate engineer teams to support an infantry company on operations involving larger formations to assure immediate engineer assistance on every unit level. When the teams did not actually accompany the infantry units on their operations, they stayed in rear areas on alert so that they could be immediately airlifted to the point where they were needed. Besides destroying enemy fortifications and bunkers, those engineers assigned directly to divisions also assisted in the preparation of defensive positions, in minesweeping, and in the rapid preparation of landing zones. The airmobile concept of warfare was coming into its own in Vietnam and the use of the helicopter in tactical operations led to the development of new expedients for preparing landing sites. Beginning in January 1966 U.S. and Vietnamese forces conducted a series of operations intended to seek out and destroy the enemy in what had been his sanctuaries. It was during these operations that the procedure for constructing forward landing zones by the use of flying engineer teams was developed."

53   Operation Cedar Falls and Operation Junction City were two massive back-to-back military operations conducted during the Vietnam War designed to crush the Vietcong's stronghold in the Iron Triangle near Saigon. Operation Cedar Falls, the largest operation of the war, took place during January 1967 and involved more than 30,000 U.S. and South Vietnamese forces. It was followed by Operation Junction City, an eighty-two-day assault that began on February 22, 1967. The initial success of these operations was short lived. In his analysis of the operations for the U.S. Army many years later, Lt. Gen. Bernard William Rogers wrote: "One of the discouraging features of both Cedar Falls and Junction City was the fact that we had insufficient forces, either U.S. or South Vietnamese, to permit us to continue to operate in the Iron Triangle and War Zone C and thereby prevent the Viet Cong from returning. In neither instance were we able to

stay around, and it was not long before there was evidence of the enemy's return. Only two days after the termination of Cedar Falls, I was checking out the Iron Triangle by helicopter and saw many persons who appeared to be Viet Cong riding bicycles or wandering around on foot . . . During the cease-fire for *Tet*, 8–12 February [1968], the Iron Triangle was again literally crawling with what appeared to be Viet Cong. They could be seen riding into, out of, and within the triangle."

57 John Walker, a veteran of the 87th Engineer Battalion in Vietnam, has become a self-appointed scribe and the leading voice of support for the battalion. His Web site, http://87theng.smugmug.com, contains the best collection of photos and reflections from the battalion.

57 The Vietnam War by the numbers: 9,087,000 military personnel served on active duty during the Vietnam era between August 1965 and May 1975. Of those, 3,403,100 served in Southeast Asia (Vietnam, Laos, Cambodia, flight crews based in Thailand, and sailors in adjacent South China Sea waters). Peak troop strength in Vietnam was 543,482, on April 30, 1969.

Casualties: Hostile deaths: 47,359; Non-hostile deaths: 10,797; Total: 58,156 (including men formerly classified as MIA and Mayaguez casualties).

Wounded in action: 303,704 with 153,329 requiring hospitalization, and 75,000 severely disabled. Amputation or crippling wounds to the lower extremities were 300 percent higher than in WWII and 70 percent higher than in Korea. Multiple amputations occurred at the rate of 18.4 percent.

Draftees vs. volunteers: 648,500 or 25 percent of total forces incountry were draftees. Draftees accounted for 17,725 (30.4 percent) of combat deaths in Vietnam.

4. Dust in the Wind

65 One of the most balanced and thorough accounts of the "lobotomy era" appeared in the *Washington Post* on April 6, 1980: "Effects of the Lobotomy Era Still Linger: Benefits of Psychosurgery Still Debated by Doctors After 20 Years." The piece was the work of *Washington Post* staff writers Glenn Frankel and Stephen J. Lynton and researcher Regina Fraind. The article details the lasting impact of the work of Dr. Walter J. Freeman and his quick-and-dirty lobotomy method, which could be performed in fifteen minutes in a doctor's office without anesthesia.

68 The famous Patton slapping incidents have been widely documented. For a particularly riveting account, I recommend Charles M. Province's book *The Unknown Patton* (Random House, 1988). Chapter 8, "The Slapping Incidents: The Whole Story," is available online at www.pattonhq.com.

70 Margaret Lindorff's "PTSD symptoms in World War II Veterans" is one of the only studies to document the effects of delayed PTSD on World War II veterans. The study is available online, and Lindorff can be contacted at PO Box 11E, Monash University, Victoria, Australia, 3800. E-mail: Margaret.Lindorff@buseco.monash.edu.au.

72   The quote from Ron Kovic is from a new edition of his acclaimed book, *Born on the Fourth of July: The Long Journey Home* (Akashic Books, 2005). His current writings, "Breaking the Silence of the Night" and "The Forgotten Wounded of Iraq," can be founded at www.TruthDig.com.

75   Sally Satel's premise that many if not most soldiers claiming PTSD are just trying to game the system has been met with overwhelming criticism by medical experts and the VA. Matthew J. Friedman, MD, the executive director of the National Center for PTSD, a division of the Department of Veterans Affairs, has said that Satel's argument was based on a "misreading or inability to appreciate the meticulous process by which personal reports of combat exposure were verified by military records." The notion of veterans falsely claiming to have PTSD is also contradicted by statistics published by the U.S. Department of Veterans Affairs. In 2002, 65,154 Vietnam veterans claimed 100 percent disability for "Psychiatric and Neurological Diseases" (about 2.1 percent of the 3.14 million soldiers who served in Vietnam). A total of 202,183 Vietnam veterans claimed a partial level mental-health disability (about 6.4 percent of all Vietnam veterans).

78   The Suicide Wall of the Internet is a site developed by Alexander Paul to memorialize Vietnam veterans who have taken their own lives. For information or to register a veteran, go to www.suicidewall.com.

78   A recent study published in the *New England Journal of Medicine* found that 15 to 17 percent of Iraq vets meet the screening criteria for major depression, generalized anxiety, or PTSD. Of those, only 23 to 40 percent are seeking help, in large part because so many others fear the stigma of having a mental disorder.

81   A lawsuit, *Veterans for Common Sense et al. v. Peake et al.*, brought in 2007 by two veterans groups, Veterans for Common Sense and Veterans United for Truth, is seeking to force a restructuring of the veterans' medical system to better handle the growing numbers of seriously injured and mentally traumatized veterans. Of particular concern to the groups are the hundreds of thousands of returning Iraq and Afghanistan veterans suffering from post-traumatic stress disorder and traumatic brain injuries who are at the greatest risk for suicide. The lawsuit doesn't seek monetary compensation.

82   Penny Coleman, widow of a Vietnam veteran who committed suicide, and the author of *Flashback*, testified at the House Veterans Committee hearing on soldier/veteran suicide. Her testimony, reprinted here, is not only moving, it is an excellent resource for anyone who seeks to understand the full impact of PTSD:

Mr. Chairman, members of the committee, fellow panelists, good morning.
      My name is Penny Coleman. I am the widow of Daniel O'Donnell, a Vietnam veteran who came home from his war with what is now known as PTSD and subsequently took his own life. I use the term PTSD grudg-

ingly—it is the official term, but it is deeply problematic. My husband did not have a disorder. He had an injury that was a direct result of his combat experience in Vietnam. Calling it a disorder is dangerous; it reinforces the idea that a traumatically injured soldier is defective, and that idea is precisely the stigma that keeps soldiers from asking for help when they need it.

I met Daniel six months after he returned from Vietnam and I married him a year later. The man I fell in love with was gentle, and playful, and very funny—on good days. But there were others when he would fly into rages over trifles, and more than a few nights when he would wake up screaming and sweating, and fighting something terrible that wasn't there. Or he would take to his bed with the blinds drawn, sometimes for days and all he would tell me was that he didn't want to live. I thought that if I loved him enough, I could fix him. I was wrong. I had no idea what I was up against. After Daniel died, I tried to blame him, but ended up blaming myself.

For my book, Flashback, I interviewed other women who lost loved ones to suicide in the wake of Vietnam. In addition to their grief, these women, like me, lived with guilt and shame and isolation. I now believe that our isolation was exploited to help camouflage a terrible tragedy. Unlike Agent Orange and Gulf War veterans who have never stopped demanding that the VA take responsibility for their illnesses, in the case of veteran suicides, the most logical advocates were dead. We, their widows, did not become advocates. We believed it was our fault, and we each thought we were the only one.

It is more than thirty years since the war in Vietnam ended, and still no one has any idea how many Vietnam veterans have taken their own lives because no one has ever tried to count them. The 1990 National Vietnam Veterans Readjustment Study, mandated by Congress and government, proved the syndrome now called PTSD, but never even mentioned suicide, in spite of the fact that suicide was central to every study that preceded it, including those on which it was based. No data, no proof. No proof, no problem.

The United States invaded Iraq in March of 2003, and by August, so many American soldiers had killed themselves that the Army sent a mental health advisory team to investigate. Their report confirmed a suicide rate three times greater than the statistical norm for the armed forces. It also acknowledged that one third of the psychiatric casualties being evacuated had suicide-related behaviors as part of their clinical presentation. Nonetheless, the team's conclusion was that soldiers were killing themselves for the same reasons that soldiers "typically" kill themselves: personal problems. A supplement to the report listed things that soldiers most often identified as stressors: seeing dead bodies or human remains, being attacked, or losing a friend, but the report itself only mentions marital problems, legal problems, financial problems, what they called "underde-veloped life coping skills." Translation: soldiers are dying because they are managing their lives and their affairs badly.

Every year since 2003, the suicide rate has increased and another team of military psychiatrists has been dispatched. Their conclusions are always the same: insufficient life coping skills. As recently as August, El-speth Ritchie of the Army Surgeon General's office insisted that, in spite of a suicide rate that had reached a twenty-six-year record high, Pentagon studies still haven't found a connection between soldier suicides and war.

There are various possible explanations for the Pentagon's refusal to accept that connection. One of the most compelling is budgetary. To cite just two examples: soldiers often resort to the self-medication when they are denied or discouraged from treatment, and that is commonly used to justify a dishonorable discharge, and that means that a soldier will be de-prived of health care benefits. Or VA claims that somehow more than 22,000 soldiers, most of whom had already been diagnosed with a post-traumatic stress injury or a traumatic brain injury, have been dismissed from the service with a diagnosis of "personality disorder," which is con-sidered a pre-existing condition, and therefore absolves the VA of any re-sponsibility for their future care. Such cynical cost-saving measures are devastating to the lives of soldiers and their families.

There is currently no cure for post-traumatic stress injuries. Though many learn to manage their symptoms, far too many will suffer the effects of their combat experience for the rest of their lives. They will continue to have nightmares and flashbacks. Many will continue to be hyper-vigilant and have "startle responses" that are often violent. Many will have trouble managing their anger and their relationships—for the rest of their lives. Many will try to self-medicate to help them forget, and far too many will die by their own hands. But that sad truth cannot be used as an excuse for inaction. Our soldiers and veterans need all the help they can get as soon as possible. Their psychic injuries may not be curable, but it is treatable. Their lives, and the lives of their families, can be made infinitely less dif-ficult if they are given the care and support they have earned. They can be assured that their suffering is a normal reaction to an abnormal situation; they can talk to other vets and practice compassion for themselves by feel-ing it for others; they can be taught proven techniques for managing their stress and anxiety; they can be relieved of the added burden of financial worry; all of which may help dissuade them from suicide.

This is a public health issue of monstrous proportion and I am here to bear witness to the fact that military suicides are not a new phenome-non. They are old news. This has happened before. It should never have been left to citizens to sound the alarm. The disingenuous surprise and de-nial from official sources is simply unacceptable. I am deeply concerned that the issue is being politicized, that sides are being taken, lines drawn *that make it appear as if there are two sides to this issue. There are not. There can't be. These are our soldiers, our veterans; they are also our husbands, our wives, our children, our parents, and they are dying by the thousands.*

I am grateful that CBS News has finally given us some solid numbers: 6,256 veteran suicides in one year. Those numbers are astonishing. They cannot be justified. Or ignored. Our soldiers and our veterans are not disposable, and yet that is how they are being treated. More than 6,256 veteran suicides a year. And each one of those numbers represents an individual beloved face and a life-shattering experience.

I know that Daniel came back from Vietnam with an injury that finally and directly caused his death. I believe that he decided he deserved to die because he had suffered too little, or that he wanted to die because he had suffered too much. We call his death a suicide, but I have come to believe it was either an execution, or euthanasia, or some tragic combination of the two. That continues to break my heart.

84 "The Invisible Wounds of War" is a joint project of the RAND Health and the RAND National Security Research divisions. The study can be purchased online at www.rand.org.

6. All That You Can't Be

102 The President's Commission on Care for America's Returning Wounded Warriors, chaired by Bob Dole and Donna Shalala, released its report on July 31, 2007, with six recommendations to improve access to medical care, services, and benefits for injured service members:

- Implement a patient-centered recovery plan for every seriously injured service member.
- Restructure the disability rating system.
- Improve treatment of post-traumatic stress disorder (PTSD) and traumatic brain injury (TBI).
- Increase the level of support provided to families of injured troops.
- Implement systems to ensure rapid transferal of patient information between the DoD and the VA.
- Ensure that Walter Reed Army Medical Center has necessary staffing and funding until its scheduled closure in 2011.

108 The Twenty-First Century GI Bill of Rights: A full description of the bill and its benefits is available on Senator Jim Webb's Web site at www.webb.senate.gov.

111 There are no national statistics for homeless veterans. However, according to a survey of more than 1,200 veterans conducted by the International

Union of Gospel Missions, with the populations of fifty-eight Rescue Missions nationwide, Vietnam veterans account for 42 percent of veterans seeking shelter; Korean War veterans, 10 percent; and Gulf War veterans, 10 percent.

The vast majority of these veterans served at least three years. Sixteen percent served more than seven years. Forty-nine percent served in the army, 19 percent in the navy, 18 percent in the marines, 12 percent in the air force, and 2 percent in the coast guard. Ninety-six percent of homeless veterans are male. Fifty-one percent are Caucasian, 37 percent African American, and 6 percent Hispanic.

8. Do You Remember Me?

131 August 16, 2008, Ram "Doc" Chavez detailed his long struggle for recognition in a letter to his former Redcatchers—those who served in the 199th Light Infantry Brigade. It is a touching tribute to those who stood by his side through many decades. It is also a troubling example of the bureaucratic tangle that veterans face.

Dear Redcatchers,

I want to share with you the good news that I received from my congressman recently, concerning the award of the Silver Star Medal for action in Vietnam with D 4/12 on May 7, 1968. It was submitted by Capt. James F. Dabney and approved by the Department of the US Army in April 2008.

Why did it take 40 years? If you remember on May 1 or on about that date, Harvey Lynn Cooley arrived to replace me as the Senior Medic. We spent a few days briefing him on the medical condition of the unit, and on May 5, I was supposed to hop on a chopper back to the main base camp. I decided to stay overnight and help the battalion surgeon to set up the Aid Station at the next Fire Base. On May 6, 1968, when Harvey's body arrived at the Aid Station, I requested to return to D 4/12 and replace my replacement.

So the National Records and the Department of the US Army said that, "I was NOT there." Till now, because they were right, on paper I completed my tour in the field on May 5 and was back at base, but I was there in the flesh with you guys. It took 40 years because the Army believed that it was a mistake because I had completed my tour on May 5, 1968.

Capt. Dabney's effort to recognize his troops has been a labor of love, respect, and honor, and successful with many of us. He has worked hard to bring "Honor, Respect, and Dignity" to D 4/12. And for that I give thanks to him, to be alive today, because of his military leadership 40 years ago. God Bless him and all our Redcatchers, both you and those that fell in the field of battle, I play Taps for them, every time I think of all of you.

*I was informed by my congressman's office in May, but did not re-
ceive a copy of the orders till this weekend. I did not want to say anything
until I had an official document in my hand. Those orders have arrived and
now I can share with you the honor.*

*My biggest military honor was to have served with such men as all of
you. Your friendship, your bravery, and your respect made me a better
human being. I have and will always cherish my tour with the Redcatchers, A Co. 4/12 and D Co. 4/12 and Co. C, 7th Spt. Bn. of the 199th Light
Infantry Brigade.*

With warm regards,

Ram "Doc" Chavez

134 Countless veterans still struggle to have Agent Orange exposure–related
illnesses confirmed. It has been a long and winding road to acknowledgment, and it continues today. Briefly, the timeline of Agent Orange
work and advocacy is as follows:

1978: VA director and Vietnam veteran Max Cleland announced that
the air force would conduct a twenty-five-year study of twelve hundred
pilots and chemical handlers who sprayed Agent Orange as part of Operation Ranch Hand. (Note that the study completely ignored troops on
the ground that were exposed to the rain of chemicals from the sky.)

1979: A class-action lawsuit was filed against five manufacturers of
Agent Orange.

March 1981: Jim Hopkins, a Vietnam veteran and marine, protesting the lack of medical attention for his Agent Orange–related illnesses,
drove his Jeep through the glass-front entry to the Wadsworth VA Hospital in Los Angeles, California, firing rounds from an AR-14 into pictures of Ronald Reagan and Jimmy Carter. He was taken away and died
two months later of unknown causes.

June 1981: Vietnam veterans waged a hunger strike in Washington,
D.C., which lasted fifty-three days and forced Congress to order studies
by the Centers for Disease Control of Agent Orange and PTSD.

1984: The preliminary results of the Ranch Hand study provided
evidence of a correlation between Agent Orange exposure and a variety
of illnesses, but cautioned that there was no definitive proof.

1984: The five manufacturers involved in the class-action lawsuit
offered an out-of-court settlement of $180 million, which was accepted.

1986: After spending $45 million, the Centers for Disease Control
halted its Agent Orange study, citing lack of clear documentation about
where Agent Orange had been used.

2003: The results of the twenty-five-year Ranch Hand study, which cost
$140 million, were published to harsh criticism that it was inadequate

and inaccurate and vastly underestimated the toll, in large part because it failed to account for exposure on the ground.

136 A 452-page report, released November 17, 2008, by the government's Research Advisory Committee on Gulf War Veterans' Illnesses, concluded that nearly 200,000 soldiers suffer from Gulf War syndrome, and that the government has not adequately addressed the research and treatment imperatives. "The extensive body of scientific research now available consistently indicates that Gulf War illness is real . . . and that few veterans have recovered or substantially improved with time," says the comprehensive overview. Calling it a "national obligation," the report called for a minimum expenditure of $60 million annually for Gulf War research.

10. Watch Fires Burning

165 The following is the complete statement by Jerry Donnellan, director of the Rockland County Veterans Service Agency, New York, New York, before the House Committee on Veterans' Affairs, Subcommittee on Disability Assistance and Memorial Affairs, October 9, 2007:

Ever been to war? Mine was in the last century and that's hard to admit. The fact we lost is even harder. Being shot at tends to focus you, and things experienced stay with you. No one hates war more than those who have lived it, yet we send our children to go and peer into hell. They come back with scars, some physical, more mental. You can't take someone from a normal ordered society and drop them into a combat zone, a year later pull them out, put them back on Main Street, and expect them not to have some baggage. In a strange way the lucky ones with all their fingers and toes can carry deeper scars. As scary as it is, you're never more alive than in combat. Your senses are on overload, pores wide open, adrenalin coursing. But you will pay for this dance with the devil, in the silence of a future midnight when the demons return to collect. Old soldiers have passed many such midnights. For us it's normal. The mission is to let this generation know that it can and must be dealt with or it will deal with you. This mission for some has become a career.

Fifty-four counties across this state have Veterans' offices. These were put in place by the State of New York in 1945 to inform returning war veterans of their rights and benefits. Makes sense because dealing with the state and federal bureaucracies is daunting. They're hard to deal with, so hard in fact that they won't release discharges and contact information on veterans returning to their counties. When questioned, we're told it's to protect the privacy of the returning veteran . . . Yep, that was my question. If we don't talk to them, who will? And do you really believe we aren't going to protect their privacy? We are of the same faith. We've shared the same baptism of fire . . .

Might be that we are too good at what we do. And giving us the contact information would allow us to reach all the returning vets in our county, that would lead to more claims, therefore, and even the larger backlog. Maybe that's the problem. Well, we shouldn't worry because these new veterans are above average. They're above average in unemployment, alcoholism, divorce, foreclosures, post-traumatic stress.

This year the Army set a record. Some say the highest in twenty-six years, others say the highest since Vietnam. The record is for suicide. But I digress. We don't have to worry about them filling out claims, but it may be a barometer. However, keeping the claims process long and frustrating saves money. First, by not having to hire more and competent people. Second, by frustrating veterans to the point where they drop their claims, there's another savings. Third, is the truly uncooperative veteran who dies while waiting for a settlement—sad, but yet another savings.

So let's get this straight. We have a government agency that's figured out that by spending less money they can make or at least keep more money. The bean counters love this stuff. So where is the motivation for change unless money in the VA budget is specifically targeted? How did we get here? Wasn't hard. We're about where we were in Vietnam. Then the VA hospital system was gearing up to handle the geriatric population of WW I when it was hit with thousands of young veterans with nasty wounds that had never been seen before. But due to advances in medical technology and speed of evacuation from the field, more of them were coming home. At that time for every person killed, three to four were wounded. If you were wounded and made it to a dust off chopper, odds were that you had a 95 percent chance of living. They didn't know what to do with them, but they did have bed space, as did the Department of Defense, so they could hang onto them longer until they figured it out.

What happens after a war in general is military and VA budgets tank. The people are tired of war, the economy is in need of transition. However, after Vietnam you could square that. It's kind of like the perfect storm in the way those three elements came together. It was a lousy war that we lost. The public was suffering not from war fatigue, they were genuinely angry and the economy was going over the falls. Remember the gas lines? So a new phrase came into our lexicon: "base closures." However, with every base at least one hospital was lost. At the same time, the VA hospitals began following the medical trend of the private sector— going into shorter hospital stays, more out-patient. Therefore, they, too, were eliminating beds and opening community clinics, the first of which was in Rockland County.

Then there was Desert Storm. That showed America we could go to the other side of the world, win a war in a hundred hours, take only one hundred and sixty-eight killed, and come home. Perfect. We avenged Vietnam and proved the bean counters right, all in one shot. It was then that the bed letting began. From the time of Desert Storm to the beginning of Iraqi freedom, the Department of Defense and Veterans Affairs beds went down 65 percent. So now we've got fewer beds especially in the Department of Defense, and now the killed-to-wounded ratio has gone off the map. For every one person killed, fifteen are wounded. We are approaching 4,000 killed in Iraq and Afghanistan. That translates to 60,000 wounded. With that number of wounded in Vietnam, we would have had 20,000 killed.

So you can see the volume has been turned way up. The wounds are more grievous and are taking longer to recover as well. Now what happens is the wounded come back to Walter Reed, Bethesda or other DOD hospitals. They can't handle the load. If DOD determines that the vet is too badly wounded to return to duty, the vet is in fact no longer of any value to the military, and he is retired. This hands the veteran off to the Department of Veterans Affairs. Not only getting them off their hands, but off their books. The VA is not in that much better shape in terms of beds and has only one-tenth of DOD's budget. Also this is the point at which VA claims begin, again adding to the backlog. VA only has so much space and so many people in terms of rehab. When new wounded come in to begin rehab, the old have no place to go. So they are sent either home to ill-equipped parents or spouses, or moved to nursing facilities.

In either case, rehabilitation effectively stops or at least considerably slows. The fact that the veterans aren't rehabilitated to the highest point possible means they become more of a burden to the VA. Again, more claims and for a longer period of time, not to mention that the veterans are left with a poorer quality of life. What could happen is DOD could hold onto these people on active duty. They would then still have Tri-care military health insurance. The veteran then could be outsourced to a state of the art private rehab facility near their home. Tri-care would be used to cover the cost. No new hospitals would need to be built or medical staff hired. And that rehab could start today and continue 'til it was determined by a medical professional, not an administrator, that as much as possible had been done for the veteran. On the claims backlog side, we could rehire recently retired claims adjudicators on a per diem or contract basis, possibly even with an incentive for more than average number of claims cleared. These people already know the system. They already have the training. There's no adjusting period. They could start tomorrow. Four of such people working full-time in each VA Regional Office could clear the backlog in two years.

The second idea would allow regular VA doctors in hospitals and clinics to diagnose vets beginning their claim, and have that diagnosis be adjudicated. The way it works now is, in order to file the claim the veteran has to have a diagnosis. That diagnosis is submitted with the claim. Months

go by, the veteran is then sent for another physical examination and di-
agnosis. In many cases, they are sent back to exactly the same medical fa-
cility and the same doctor who examined them in the first place.
Therefore, if the original doctor is a VA doctor, let them submit their find-
ings directly to the adjudication board. This may necessitate an increase
in doctors on the clinic level, however one doctor could serve several clin-
ics. That in itself should take a couple of months out of the claim process.
It's not perfect, or may not work in all circumstances, but I'll take a bite.
These people, facilities, and systems are all in place as we speak. This
could begin tomorrow if there is a political will to do so.

Lastly, appoint someone to head up the transition, who would report
back to Congress in six months. Max Cleland would be my suggestion. As
a former senator he knows the beltway. As the former Director of the Vet-
erans Administration under President Carter, he knows the VA. As a
wounded Vietnam veteran he has seen the system from both sides.

166 In late 2003, there was hardly a mention in the media of the hundreds
     of wounded and disabled soldiers being warehoused in dilapidated
     World War II–era barracks at Fort Knox, Kentucky, or the hundreds more
     at Fort Stewart, Georgia, who were forced to live in squalor while waiting
     months for medical treatment. Leaking roofs, rodent infestation, lack of
     air-conditioning during the hottest months of summer, filthy latrines,
     and substandard care met these returning soldiers, who were even asked
     to pay for their own toilet paper. Until Congress intervened, they were
     also charged $8.10 a day for meals.

166 Greg Mitchell, editor of *Editor and Publisher* magazine, and the author of
     *So Wrong for So Long: How the Press, the Pundits—and the President—Failed
     in Iraq*, has documented press coverage of the war, including the period
     leading up to the invasions of Afghanistan and Iraq. Mitchell holds up a
     bright light of accountability to the media for its lackluster reporting on
     the war, especially as the years pass. Press negligence translates to pub-
     lic negligence. Indeed, prior to Election Day 2008, only 10 percent of
     those polled said they considered the Iraq War a primary issue.

INDEX

—